DESIGNING SPECIAL PROGRAMMES

Tony Branwhite

DESIGNING SPECIAL PROGRAMMES

A handbook for
teachers of children
with learning difficulties

Methuen · London

First published in 1986 by
Methuen & Co. Ltd
11 New Fetter Lane,
London EC4P 4EE

© 1986 Tony Branwhite

Set by Hope Services,
Abingdon, Oxon.
Printed in Great Britain by
Richard Clay (The Chaucer Press),
Bungay, Suffolk

British Library Cataloguing in
Publication Data

Branwhite, Tony
Designing special programmes: a
handbook for teachers of children
with learning difficulties.
1. Slow learning children –
Great Britain
2. Remedial teaching
I. Title
371.92' 6'0941   LC4696.G7

ISBN 0 416 91930 8
      0 416 42040 0 Pbk

d 652(1) 10 · 86

They cannot read, and so don't lisp in criticism;
Nor write, and so they don't affect the muse:
Were never caught in epigram or witticism,
Have no romances, sermons, plays, reviews.

(Lord Byron)

To children in the special-
needs population, for whom
the above words might
aptly have been written
and from whom we have
so much to learn.

Contents

Preface

This handbook is about some of the instructional issues underlying the design of learning programmes for 'low-ability' children, or children with special needs, a topic of both social and professional relevance for the education service, since the quest for higher standards of design has become a widespread pursuit in today's society. Although it may be chic in select circles to have this exemplified in, say, a car designed by Bertone, shoes by Gucci, or clothing by Dior, it has in reality become a commonplace expectation that most of the things we use will be well designed. With the development of original colours, the increased blending of shapes, the exploitation of new materials, and faster communications, advanced design techniques have created fresh potential in many areas of human activity. One interesting consequence of this trend has been that the British Government has sponsored an institution in London known as 'the Design Council', which awards an official seal of approval to new products that exemplify good design. However, while there is a comparable public expectation of design excellence in education, no central agency exists to provide a seal of approval for it in learning programmes.

There can be little doubt that a demand for well-designed learning programmes is present, if for no other reason than that it is estimated that up to 20 per cent of the British school population require assistance beyond that to be found in the normal curriculum. As if this were not sufficient justification, it will be evident to most teachers that children in this group are less likely to remedy their own problems unaided and frequently have to be taught skills which other children acquire for themselves. It has also been said (Strain and Shores, 1983) that an absence of skill is associated with an absence of instruction, and that humanitarian concern for the well-being of children is shown directly in teaching terms by the provision of appropriate instruction. The issue of how this may best be formulated for children with persistent learning difficulties is clearly worth close attention.

Acknowledgements

The author would like to thank Professor Alan Clarke and Professor Ann Clarke, of the University of Hull, for their constructive criticisms of the initial draft of the manuscript, and would like to express gratitude to Professor Klaus Wedell, of the University of London, for his comments and advice on a later draft. Various helpful suggestions from immediate colleagues and friends were also much appreciated. He would also like to acknowledge the kindness shown by Professor Douglas Carnine and associates at the University of Oregon, and likewise that of Professor Tom Lovitt and associates at the University of Washington. Appreciation is also expressed to the staff of the Brynmor Jones Library, University of Hull, for their helpful assistance, and to Jean Parr, Heather Nicholson and Diana Barnes for careful preparation of the typescript.

The author and the publishers would like to thank the following copyright holders for permission to reproduce material: John Wiley & Sons for Figure 1; Irvington Publishers, Inc. for Figure 3 and Fastcheck 25; Charles E. Merrill Publishing Company for material in Fastcheck 16; Croom Helm Ltd for computer dialogue in Fastcheck 29.

Introduction

A brave new world for special education was heralded by the implementation of the 1981 Education Act, an important development in British legislation, which set out to make provision for children with special educational needs. As a result of changes in educational philosophy proposed earlier in the Warnock Report, it abolished at a stroke the use of set administrative labels which had formed the basis for making categorical placement decisions. These were replaced in law by the broader but somewhat tautologous view that special educational need existed where 'learning difficulties' were present which required provision for special education. The existence of a learning difficulty was then enshrined in the legal definition that a child 'has a significantly greater difficulty in learning than the majority of children of his age', or 'a disability which either prevents or hinders him from making use of educational facilities of a kind generally provided in school.'

The advice that came from the Department of Education and Science through Circular 1/83 was, in principle, that the assessment of a child's learning difficulties should distinguish between the stages of analysis, specification of the child's need, and determination of the appropriate measures to meet the existing need. Accordingly, professional advice was to be offered regardless of the eventual school placement to be made for the child, a radical departure from previous practice which was geared towards fitting the child into a segregated school system. While Local Education Authorities were directed to provide guidance for all their schools regarding the identification of special needs, assessment procedures, and advice on the specialist services available, it followed that the central task of education professionals became that of carrying out assessments based on need prior to any change of provision, and later meeting the needs as specified once a placement decision had been carried out.

One consequence of this legislation has been an increase in the level of demand upon teachers' professional competence, partly because of a shift towards non-categorical placement and partly as a result of public attention continuing to focus upon the issue of integration. With moves towards a less segregated approach to children with special needs, more teachers than ever before can expect to come into contact with children from that sector of the school population. However, a 1983 survey of 130 teacher-training institutions by the Royal Society for Disability and Rehabilitation revealed that at least half the students in teacher training received no instruction at all on how to teach children with special needs in mainstream schools. Therefore some teachers will not have been given an adequate background for this task, and many more may be reliant on the thoroughgoing organization of in-service training by their LEA.

A particular demand faced by teachers, adequately prepared or not, is that they are now expected to help overcome learning difficulties by means of relevant educational programmes. The Department of Education and Science has stated that responsibility for the planning of detailed programmes lies with teachers (Circular 1/83; paragraph 38), and this is in line with educational practice in the United States and Canada. Since the passage of Public Law 94–142 in 1975, teachers in the USA, for example, have been obliged to contribute to what is known as an 'Individualized Education Programme' (IEP) for every special-needs child, to include the following components:

1 Details of the child's present performance.

2 Long- and short-term goals specifying what is to be learned *and* how it will be taught.
3 An outline of services to meet the child's needs, dates from which they will be in place, and the expected time for which they will continue.
4 Evaluation criteria for determining the efficacy of the IEP.

A similar orientation has been adopted in Canada, where the Ontario Government's 'Bill '82' makes it mandatory that every 'exceptional' child be provided with an individual programme based on specific educational objectives and is protected by a plan listing the services intended to fulfil these objectives. While the laudable aim of formulating effective programmes is approached with slightly differing emphases in each of these two countries, it is difficult to envisage just how the legal requirements could be met in any one of them without very carefully structured input from teachers.

While it is presumed that British teachers will plan learning programmes, then, in the absence of official guidelines to indicate just what is meant by the term 'programme', any teacher wishing to make the appropriate professional response must seek definition elsewhere. One convenient source of reference is provided by dictionaries, and in general usage a programme is taken to be a schedule or plan of procedure, 'a definite plan of intended proceedings', as *The Concise Oxford Dictionary* puts it. A somewhat more educational definition is given in the *OED Supplement*, which refers to 'the establishment of learning-patterns through the stimulus of rewarding correct responses or behaviour at each step'. However, this seems to confuse the meaning of stimulus and reinforcement, and clearly derives from the 1960s era of teaching-machines and programmed learning. In the same vein, *Chambers' Twentieth Century Dictionary* lists 'a course of instruction by book or teaching-machine, in which subject matter is broken down into a logical sequence of short items of information', and this is in some ways clearer. Neither of these alternatives directly involves teachers, but *Webster's International Dictionary* apparently does allow scope for teacher action, by referring to a programme as 'a schedule or system under which actions can be taken to a desired goal', and 'a plan of study for an individual student over a given period'.

In today's educational climate, these definitions seem either restrictive or out-of-date, and none of them appears to offer a stand-alone capability. Few teachers indeed would be content to rest with just a plan, or work only through books or teaching-machines, or focus solely upon an individual child. As a rule, teachers not only plan, but also use a diversity of materials and techniques to transform the way in which a variety of children function. To achieve a workable definition, it is necessary to take existing practice into account, hence a blend of the above features seems more relevant, and suggests that, in dealing with children having special learning needs, one possible definition of the term 'programme' might be as follows: *A multi-sensory teaching system of short interactive sequences designed to transform learning performance.* Thus a premium is placed upon *teaching* functions, which systematically link information and learning activities in more than one form, to enhance the way in which the learner operates.

Although the above definition is relatively broad, note that it is not so broad that 'programme' becomes synonymous with 'curriculum'. By this definition, a programme is something less than a total statement defining all of the educational activities which a school may provide, and it is only a part of the means whereby the values of a culture are transmitted to children. These are qualities of the curriculum in its fullest sense, as recently outlined by HM Inspectorate in a discussion document ('The Curriculum from 5 to 16', HMSO, 1985). Specific learning programmes could therefore be taken as contributing to particular elements of the curriculum.

By the same token, this definition would not mean that all educational activities would qualify as a learning programme. Approaches based exclusively on 'chalk and talk' by the teacher, or independent activity by the child, would be excluded, as would some apparently more structured tactics. Take, for example, a series of teaching targets expressed as a sequence of tasks:

TASK 1: Subtract units from a total of 2.
TASK 2: Subtract units from a total of 3.

responsibility and the question of how to fulfil it will no doubt be present in many teachers' minds. Considerable forethought would seem to be required, although teachers are, of course, frequently advised to work in an organized manner. Walkin (1982), for instance, proposed that lesson plans should be written out in a logical sequence, incorporating a variety of activities, frequent checks on learning and details of methods or aids to be used. Although several broad outlines of this kind are available, evidently they do not go so far as to constitute detailed guidance on the production of learning programmes. Indeed, some sources which purport to cover the topic of programme design for children with special needs provide virtually no relevant guidance to the systematic organization and presentation of learning programmes.

Apart from an Open University course, which is limited to the design of computer software (P541: Educational Software), in this important new area specific advice for teachers seems to be in short supply. A current 'special need' therefore involves the search for practical directions regarding programme construction, implementation and evaluation, and three potential avenues will be explored here. These include teacher-based, learner-based and programme-based issues, with the greatest emphasis on those which are programme-based.

This text is founded on an up-to-date review of original sources in educational literature, which represent a careful selection of recent research findings and promising techniques available from current practice. Attempts have been made throughout to keep the material relevant to issues commonly encountered in helping children with special learning needs and the author hopes that teachers involved in this work will find ideas in the text which are constructive from the point of view of their own endeavours.

1
The abilities
of the teacher

One has only to pick up a national newspaper or tune in to a current affairs broadcast on radio or television to realize that quite a lot of public debate about teaching is taking place, some of which has generated rather more heat than light. Apart from this, however, educational researchers have for some time been attempting to make a somewhat cooler and more thoughtful assessment and substantial research effort has been invested in attempting to discover what helps teachers to become more effective. Much of this has dealt with personality characteristics or other individual traits, such as intellectual achievement, age or length of service. Bloom (1980), however, pointed out that all this bears a very poor relationship to pupil achievement (correlations below 0.20), so the short answer seems to be that what makes teachers effective is the obvious quality of their teaching. Perhaps it is possible after all that good teachers are made as well as born!

Task-related factors seem to provide a more fruitful source for understanding factors that contribute to effective teaching. For example, Brophy and Evertson (1977) found that successful teachers of low-ability children bring a high degree of organization to their work, and Bloom (1968) summarized research on effective teaching as highlighting four important outcomes (Fastcheck 1).

Fastcheck 1	Four parameters of effective teaching
	1 Give a clear description of the learning task. 2 Specify for the children how they should respond. 3 Practise the responses called for until they are learned. 4 Link reinforcement procedures to the learning process.

(After Bloom, 1968)

There is also something to be said for starting in the way in which you mean to go on, for Emmer, Evertson and Anderson (1980) were able to distinguish between more effective and less effective teachers within the early weeks of the school year. They found that the more effective teachers, while varying as individuals, were generally better organized. Classroom routines were established early, often taught step-by-step, and the children monitored to verify that they responded appropriately. Directions were given clearly, and written on the board, children were provided with follow-on activities to keep them busy at the end of assignments, and transitions between tasks were kept brief and were smoothly executed. These teachers prevented problems from occurring by carefully worked-out systems for planning instruction.

In an extensive review of teaching procedures that promote mastery of skills, Rosenshine (1979) recorded that the teachers who made a difference to learning achievement were those who established and sustained contact between the learner and the curriculum materials. He also concluded that the more success-ful teacher was the one who structured learning, and led and supervised teaching groups, making the most of the time spent in on-task activity. Good and Brophy (1984) supported these conclusions.

Time-on-task, now sometimes termed 'engaged time', is a useful concept in that it helps us to discriminate between two important features of academic learning time (ALT): firstly, the amount of time allocated to a given area of the curriculum and, secondly, the amount of time actually used productively by the children. Time-on-task relates to the latter. These variables have sometimes both been included under ALT but in fact each represents a different facet of it. It is easy to allocate, say, a forty-minute period to some specific learning activity but whether the children actually work for all of the time available is an open question and some studies have shown that a surprising amount of classroom time is lost as far as learning is concerned. Clearly, the more meaningful variable from the point of view of children's progress is that of time-on-task.

Kounin and Gump (1974) analysed nearly 600 hours of video-taped classroom teaching and found that frequent cues from the teacher promoted more involvement by the pupil with the task at hand, and this is in keeping with the findings of other researchers (Good and Beckerman, 1978; Fisher *et al.*, 1978) that teacher-led instruction increases on-task activity on the part of the children. On the same note, Emmer and Evertson (1980) concluded that one advantage of teacher-led group instruction over individual seatwork assignments was that a continuous flow of cues from the teacher steered children towards greater involvement in their task at hand. When children are working on their own, the teacher just does not have the same degree of control over the cues to which they respond. A small-scale study by Darch and Gersten (1985) suggests that more progress can occur when children are moved straight on to a new task by their teacher immediately they have finished an activity already at hand, and are given appropriate praise. The combined effect of a rapid pace and specific teacher praise was more powerful than either variable used separately in this study.

The flow of communication also affects the level of involvement between child and learning task. Anderson (1984, p. 149) indicated that one-way communication from teacher to children (e.g. a lecture) is associated with reduced levels of time-on-task for pupils of lower verbal ability. Teaching methods which provide two-way communication (e.g. which is largely teacher-directed but which encourages children to participate by giving answers and asking questions) are associated with relatively high levels of time-on-task for all types of children.

Given that wholly individual instruction for every child can be so difficult to organize in reality as to be generally impractical, a review by Stevens and Rosenshine (1981) characterizes effectively set-up instruction by the four main variables set out in Fastcheck 2.

Fastcheck 2

Four features of effective instructional settings
1 Effective instruction takes place in group settings. 2 Effective instruction is teacher-directed. 3 Effective instruction is academically focused. 4 Effective instruction is individualized.

(After Stevens and Rosenshine, 1981)

In a large-scale analysis of research on the relationship between group size and achievement outcomes Glass and Smith (1978) reported that greater achievement results from teaching *small* groups of children. Although some technical controversy arose over their study, the importance of this finding for children with significant learning difficulties has not been disputed. Forness and Kavale (1985) have also reported a study of twenty-six special classes in which they found that children in small teaching groups consistently had more opportunity for communication than peers placed in larger groups.

Stevens and Rosenshine (1981) indicated that teaching to groups of children promoted more on-task activity than did an emphasis on assignments for the individual; also, that teacher demonstration, corrective feedback, and increased practice through choral responding became more evenly available by this means. Teachers who promoted the greatest achievement gains were business-like and centred learning activity around themselves, against less successful teachers, who tended to take a back seat and follow the children's lead. The belief that techniques allowing children to direct the course of their own learning are as valid for those with special needs as their normal peers might well require revision in the light of these findings.

Evidence from seven substantial studies led Stevens and Rosenshine to the view that effective teachers spent optimal time working on core curriculum areas, and frequently checked children's performance. Improvement of educational performance through discussion of children's feelings was found to be ineffective in these studies. Likewise, individualized learning was judged to be inefficient where it emphasized the child directing his or her own work but it was useful where initial teacher-led instruction helped each child towards later independent activity.

Stevens and Rosenshine (1981) described the basic teaching procedure for promoting learner competence as *'Demonstration-Prompt-Practice'*. This begins with a demonstration of how the learner should respond to the skill or rule selected, then enters a period of supervised practice of the various activities being taught, with accompanying prompts and corrections by the teacher and, finally, provides time for independent practice. When mistakes occur in the final phase, the demonstration and supervised practice phases are repeated (see Fastcheck 3).

Lest it might be thought that research suggests that it is important to be committed to work and nothing else in order to be successful as a teacher, this is most certainly not the case! Empathic qualities are also of great importance and a pertinent observation was made by Wragg (1984), who, in referring to the approach of experienced teachers with new classes, noted that a number introduced humour early on in the school year, contrary to the popular advice not to smile until Christmas! That leadership and humanity in the classroom act in a complementary fashion is a view supported by recent research on affective aspects of different teaching regimes. (Children have a right to be treated like human beings!)

Medley (1979) is in agreement with other reviewers in commenting that the effective teacher maintains both academic activity and psychological support in the classroom. This view is supported by Solomon and Kendall (1979), who reported that criticism, shouting, scolding, ridicule and sarcasm exercise an adverse effect on achievement. They found that in fact this kind of input did not feature significantly among teachers and pupils where the emphasis was on academic learning tasks conducted in a supportive classroom atmosphere. Likewise, a study by Filby and Cahen (1977) concluded that teachers who upheld a strong task-orientation also tended to be well informed about children as individuals, i.e. their professional

Fastcheck 3	**Using demonstration–prompt–practice**
	1 To help teach her class of 7-year-olds cursive writing, Mrs Ellis has a model of each letter displayed on the classroom wall.
	2 For formation purposes she states the following rules:
	2.1 Start at the green dot.
	2.2 Follow the arrow.
	2.3 Stop at the red dot.
	3 She writes a given letter on the board, one element at a time, following the above conventions.
	4 The children complete a worksheet which involves tracing the letter and which gives the necessary formation cues.
	5 Mrs Ellis checks the result and shows the children how to correct any errors, guiding their hands if necessary.
	6 When the worksheet is completed correctly, each child then has to write a page of the letter concerned in a copywriting book.
	7 If more than three errors per line occur in the copywriting book, Mrs Ellis gives the child a repeat worksheet assessment.

commitment was apparent at both task and personal levels.

This investigation also produced a rather intriguing finding, for Filby and Cahen's data revealed that the weakest gains in achievement actually related to situations in which teachers specifically highlighted personal factors and played down the emphasis on learning. Similarly, in the United States Office of Education very large-scale 'Follow Through' project, educational programmes which set out to reduce the amount of structure in classroom learning and to reinforce personal responsibility, paradoxically had least effect on increasing children's self-esteem ratings. Children who had been in such programmes actually had lower scores on the Coopersmith Self-Esteem Inventory than peers who had participated in programmes which sought to develop mainly academic skills.

In essence, the message from this kind of research appears to be that increasing a child's level of competence in basic educational skills contributes towards him developing a more positive image of himself. As such it represents a significant advance over previously held ideas on developing self-concept, described by Coopersmith and Feldman (1974) as offering freedom without imposed limits. Special-needs children can benefit from having clear educational constraints within which to operate, such as classroom events that have predictable features which facilitate learning and help them to develop self-respect. Possibly the process of informal comparison between children, in terms of whether they can or cannot manage certain learning tasks, is the one that links classroom performance to self-image, by means of the child's own idea of his social status within his current peer group. Any child who repeatedly fails to master skills which have been learned by his peers may then be exposed to the risk that they use his failure as an extra ground for personal criticism. By the same token, a child who has been helped to acquire the relevant set of skills through careful teaching is freed from such performance-related criticism, and can be confident that he compares favourably with other children. This is not to say that the curriculum should focus solely upon basic-skills instruction, of course, but this does seem to produce certain benefits, not the least of which is that it can help to provide a foundation for developing a much wider range of understanding and knowledge later on.

A number of the qualities discussed above have been drawn together by Bell and Kerry (1982, p. 54) in the form of a twelve-item checklist as set out in Fastcheck 4. It can thus be seen that there is substantial research support for a view that should be professionally appealing – that by being firm, humane, and providing effective guidance, teachers can become the key to children's success. From this it is but a small step to recognizing that programme design must take into account teaching procedures which include the modelling of responses, monitoring the learner during practice, reinforcing accurate responses, and correcting errors, tactics which are familiar in some form to most teachers already working with special-needs children. In addition, such teaching procedures are clearly compatible with Feuerstein's (1980) notion of the *Mediated*

Fastcheck 4

Management clues from effective British teachers
FOR COMMUNICATION: Speak clearly and give careful instructions. Give praise and encouragement.
FOR LEARNING: Plan lessons at an appropriate level. Be sensitive to individual learning needs. Assign a high priority to basic skills and life skills. Have presentation skills which keep the classroom interesting and lively.
FOR BEHAVIOUR: Make good relationships with children as individuals. Show consistent attitudes about classroom behaviour. Keep steady but friendly discipline. Be aware of pupils' changing emotional states. Have a patient manner. Keep a sense of humour.

(After Bell and Kerry, 1982, p.54)

learning experience, which goes beyond a simple stimulus–response model of learning. Feuerstein's view is that in mediating between the stimulus material and the child, a teacher helps him or her to acquire appropriate behaviours, learning sets, and ways of working sooner than would otherwise be possible. The earlier that *Mediated* learning experiences begin, he argues, the greater the child's capacity for further learning and development (see Fastcheck 5).

Fastcheck 5

Helping a reader of low fluency by demonstration and practice

1 ASSUMPTIONS:
   1.1 The existence of a reasonable level of decoding skills
   1.2 Text presented at the child's instructional level.
   1.3 The presence of a fluent tutor.

2 READING PROCEDURES:
   2.1 The tutor makes a brief introductory comment, such as, 'We are going to work together to help you read a little better', so that the child knows what the goal is.
   2.2 Tutor indicates the first sentence and says 'Listen; I'll read it carefully', then reads it *slowly* with appropriate pauses and inflections.
   2.3 Tutor says, 'Listen again', then reads the sentence at the *normal* rate with appropriate pauses and inflections.
   2.4 Tutor says, 'Read it with me', then child and tutor read it together.
   2.5 Tutor says, 'Now *you* read it with expression', and has child read the sentence.
   2.6 Tutor says, 'Once more' and has child repeat the sentence.
   2.7 Tutor says, 'Good reading with expression' or gives similar praise.
   2.8 On sentence 2, tutor repeats steps 2.2 through 2.7.
   2.9 At sentence 3, tutor omits model, going straight to 'Read it with me.'
   2.10 At sentence 4, tutor omits supervised practice, going to: 'Now *you* read it with expression.' From this point on, the tutor's task is to supply verbal recognition for good performance, and correction of errors.

3 CORRECTIONS:
   3.1 To correct a *miscue*, when the child reads something inaccurately the tutor immediately says the word correctly, and asks the child to repeat it.
   3.2 To correct a *lack of expression*, when the child misses punctuation marks or an important inflection the tutor says, 'Listen to *me* read it with expression', and does so *emphasizing* the relevant expression. The tutor then asks the child to attempt that section again.

4 SYNOPSIS:

	SENTENCE NUMBER			
	1	2	3	4 to end
MODEL (TUTOR)	√	√		
SHADOW (TUTOR AND CHILD)	√	√	√	
PRACTICE (CHILD)	√	√	√	√
CORRECT (TUTOR)	√	√	√	√

Review one

DIRECTIONS

To check the extent of your understanding at this point, it is recommended that you attempt to answer all ten questions in the review *before* you look up any of the answers supplied. All of the questions are derived from the text but you may find some a little harder than the others. You are specifically advised against reading later sections of the text until you have completed this review.

REVIEW QUESTIONS

1 Do successful teachers of low-ability children tend to be highly organized in their work or not?
2 Are the concepts of time allocated and time-on-task synonymous with each other?
3 Which is the more meaningful variable for measuring learning progress, time allocated or time-on-task?
4 What kind of teacher communication is most closely associated with higher levels of time-on-task, one-way or two-way?
5 What size of teaching group leads to most achievement for low-ability children: large, small or medium?
6 Which is likely to yield more on-task activity for the learner, small-group teaching or independent seatwork?
7 Do teachers who promote greatest achievement gains typically centre learning activity around themselves, or follow the children's lead?
8 Should practice sessions come before a demonstration or afterwards?
9 In what direction is learning performance affected by an emotionally austere classroom regime?
10 Is an emphasis on personal responsibility alone likely to produce a sustained improvement in the quality of children's work?

GUIDELINES

After attempting all ten questions, compare your responses

with the answers given for this purpose. An acceptable mastery level for Review One is nine answers correct. It is suggested that you look through the text related to any incorrect responses. (Page numbers are listed against the answers in the Answers to Reviews section, pages 141–6, to help you do this quickly.) If you have less than eight answers correct, it is likely that you will profit from re-reading the preceding section for a fuller understanding.

2
The abilities
of the child

Ability, in the sense employed here, derives from a profile of performance attributes as identified by normative tests (those tests which compare an individual's performance to that of a peer group; so that a child with a reading age of 7 is typically thought to read like average 7-year-olds) and is an almost universally familiar concept in education. Blankenship and Lilley (1981) pointed out that advocates of ability-based approaches to teaching claim that when children fail to learn, it is because they possess some underlying deficiency which must be corrected. The deficiency is usually defined in terms of a set of psychological processes and the argument appears to be that, until the deficiency is made good, the lack of the relevant skills will not be remedied; i.e. a *causal* relationship between underlying, or covert, process and an evident, or overt, skill is implied, even though the process is essentially a hypothetical construct.

Although Bryant and Bradley (1979) commented that it was psychologists who worried about underlying processes and forgot to look at children's reading skills directly, while educationalists certainly stuck to real reading but did not look very far into what lay beneath it, the suggestion that learning difficulties derive from an admixture of strong or weak psychological processes persists and, for reading, has virtually

Fastcheck 7

Conclusions regarding the training of basic abilities	
ASSUMPTION	CONCLUSION
1 Educationally relevant psychological abilities exist and can be measured.	Such abilities are not directly observable and must be inferred from behaviour. They are impossible to refute, since failure to detect their presence could in reality be attributed to the technical inadequacy of present-day tests. (Of course, this argument cuts both ways, as by the same logic detection could also be in error.)
2 Existing tests used in differential diagnosis are reliable.	Reliabilities of many instruments are too low to justify confidence in them. While it may be possible that isolated sub-tests are more reliable for specific purposes, this has yet to be demonstrated.
3 Existing tests used for differential diagnosis are valid.	Reviews on construct validity provide mixed results. Except for auditory tests, diagnostic validity is inadequate. Predictive validity is limited by the lack of reliability which is a common deficiency in this field.
4 Prescriptions can be generated from differential diagnosis to remedy weak abilities.	A review of 100 studies covering auditory, visual and psycholinguistic programmes yielded little supporting evidence. It is difficult to escape the conclusion that abilities measured in differential diagnosis are unlikely to be improved by existing training procedures.
5 The remedying of weak abilities improves achievement.	When results on reading and general achievement are analysed by type of training programme, the results fail to support any particular approach to ability training. In the majority of studies, control groups performed as well on both ability and academic measures as did the experimental groups.
6 Prescriptions can be generated from ability profiles to improve academic achievement with no direct training of weak abilities.	The consistently negative nature of these results casts considerable doubt on the usefulness of ability assessments in planning academic instruction. However, modality studies to date have been concerned with reading instruction; other academic areas may be more sensitive to modality influence.

(After Arter and Jenkins, 1979)

went through a substantial body of research and were able to find fourteen experimental studies which were well designed. Of this number, thirteen of the studies revealed that children were not normally helped to read by instruction that matched their modality strengths. The single exception applied to comprehension skills in 16-year-olds. Tarver's (1978) review similarly concluded that 'the evidence indicates that modality preference and method of teaching reading do not interact significantly when we are concerned with actual methods of teaching reading and measures of reading achievement'.

Ysseldyke and Algozzine (1980) warned that a contributory factor could be the technical inadaquacy of diagnostic tests, which can lack either adequate reliability, the necessary validity or, indeed, both. (Technically inadequate tests may deliver a false picture of how well or how badly a child is coping, either by underestimating or overstating his level of performance.) Jenkins and Pany (1978) pointed out that from a teaching point of view, there was a need for measuring instruments sensitive to differences in what was being taught, and to the developing mastery of skills in the children concerned.

Even the ubiquitous Wechsler Intelligence Scale for Children (Revised Form), widely recognized as a test which is well designed, has been criticized on these grounds. Hirschoren and Kavale (1976) stated that there was no evidence to suggest that WISC-R profiles had utility for planning remedial programmes, and Quattrochi and Sherrets (1980) reported that differences in sub-test scatter were difficult to interpret, current research indicating that even normal subjects exhibited considerable within-test variability.

This problem was put in a nutshell by Anderson, Kaufman and Kaufman (1976) in their analysis of WISC-R score differences in learning-disabled and normal children (See Fastcheck 8).

The data indicate no statistically significant differences in the range of sub-test scores between learning-disabled and normal children in their verbal, performance or full-scale scores on the WISC-R. Although the size of the discrepancy between verbal and performance scores does differ significantly between the groups, 31 per cent of the 2200 normal children in the sample obtained verbal to performance scale differences which

Fastcheck 8

Average range of WISC-R scaled score differences			
	Learning–disabled	Normal	Statistical outcome
Verbal scale	4.8	4.5	NS
Performance scale	5.7	5.5	NS
Full scale	7.5	7.0	NS
Verbal–performance differences	12.5	9.7	P < 0.05

(After Anderson, Kaufman and Kaufman, 1976)

exceeded the 12.5 point average difference for learning-disabled children. Anderson *et al.* concluded that the results of their comparison should serve as a caution for psychologists to consider the normal fluctuations in sub-test scatter when evaluating a child's score-profile on this test. Their view was reiterated by Berk (1983) who suggested that WISC-R profiles should not be used at all for the diagnosis of specific learning difficulties. Perhaps the final word to date upon this issue should be with Kavale and Forness (1985) who have carried out a rigorous scientific and philosophical analysis of the 'ability' approach to learning difficulties, and conclude that it is if anything pseudo-scientific and tantamount to an on-going professional fraud.

Tarver (1978) pointed out that since repeated attempts to assess psychological strengths and weaknesses for teaching purposes had so far met with little success, it was perhaps time to turn our attention to assessing the task to be learned. This principle was echoed by Simpson and Arnold (1983), who argued that the principal site of defective learning was not the pupil, but rather lay in the instructional procedures, a view which seems to be gaining ground in the educational research community. Indeed, Mann (1971) had already suggested the possibility that instructional variables might prove to be of greater importance than either specific process variables or individual differences. Cohen (1973) took an even stronger line, asserting that antecedent conditions which led to academic failure were usually irrelevant to educational methods.

Learning difficulties must necessarily come to light in *learning* situations. In school such a situation will occur when an interaction takes place between child and curriculum, usually involving a teacher. It is in the context of this interaction that failure to learn will initially emerge.

Now if a child becomes involved in a major road accident while out of school (another interactive situation), it would seem prudent to find out just how the factors involved interacted to bring such an unfortunate occurrence about. Evaluation conducted on a rational basis (as, for example, in a court of law) would examine the proportional effect of each interacting variable, such as the conditions under which the accident occurred, the actions of the child and the actions of other parties involved, *but this would be done in relation to pertinent traffic laws*, the 'curriculum' of the highway. By the same token then, should a child have some major 'learning accident' in school, due consideration of all the factors involved, *including the relevant curriculum background*, might judiciously be expected.

The assessment of children's ability from this point of view was applied by means of direct skill measurement in Koenig and Kunzelmann's (1980) *Classroom Learning Screening* package, and more recently exemplified in Ainscow and Tweddle's (1984) *Early Learning Skills Analysis* (ELSA). ELSA, for example, spans seven separate curriculum areas in thirty-one discrete units, covering a total of 122 performance objectives for children below 10 years of age. Using a standard ELSA format (see Figure 1), a child's performance can be assessed independently for each separate objective, or indeed any combination of them. Note that this represents classroom-valid measurement, obtained in an unambiguous manner, making it clear what is involved in terms of materials, instructions, and pupil performance, through a series of criterion-referenced tests.

Such a model of assessment necessarily goes beyond attempts to hold the child responsible for creating his own problems, the

	Materials	Instructions	Pupil performance	Recommended criteria
A6	Thirty numerals with 0 to 10 printed in random order two or three times each, presented for half a minute	'Read these numbers as quickly as you can, trying not to make any mistakes'	Reads aloud numbers 0 to 10	50 per min. Max. 2 errors
A7	Paper and pencil	'Write down these numbers as I say them', using ten numbers between 0 and 10 in random order	Writes numerals 0 to 10 from dictation	10/10
A8	Five sets of between 0 and 10 identical objects Paper and pencil	For each set 'Write down how many are here'	Writes cardinal property of sets with between 0 and 10 objects	5/5

Notes/Comments

Figure 1. The ELSA Test Format
(Ainscow and Tweddle, 1984)

important point being that assessment should not discriminate unfairly against special-needs children. Any model of assessment which is restricted to the characteristics of the child, when learning difficulties emerge from his interaction with teaching and curriculum variables, at best stands in danger of making just that mistake, and at worst represents a questionable professional ethic in an age of accountable education services.

It therefore seems reasonable to conclude that, while differential diagnosis of psychological abilities has helped to raise public and professional consciousness in the learning difficulties arena, at present it leaves something to be desired as a theoretical base for planning precise educational programmes. While there may still be some clinical applications for the ability-training model, within educational settings where the primary emphasis is placed on learning, curriculum-based assessment (CBA) would probably have more direct implications for educational practice. This may also help to reduce the irrelevance of some psychological reports to activities taking place in the classroom, as pointed out by Torgesen (1979) and, at the same time, keep programme-related decisions in the hands of teachers, who are strategically placed to implement rapid changes. By taking full account of a child's response to the curriculum, and adding this to first-hand knowledge of his or her personality, motivation, and behaviour, a teacher can respond to far more subtle variations in individual need than can possibly be derived from global estimates of ability.

Review two

DIRECTIONS:

To check the extent of your understanding at this point, it is recommended that you attempt to answer all ten questions in the review *before* you look up any of the answers supplied. All of the questions are derived from the text, but you may find some a little harder than others, so do not be surprised if you are unable to answer them all at first; just try your best with each one. You are specifically advised against reading later sections of the text until you have completed this review.

REVIEW QUESTIONS

1 Do normative tests compare a child's output with his own previous performance, or with that of other children?
2 Is a test which somehow relates performance to age a normative test?
3 Name three proposed psychological processes.
4 Are psychological processes generally held to be covert or overt?
5 Are psychological processes directly observable, or must they be inferred from the child's behaviour?
6 Are tests which are currently employed for diagnostic purposes universally reliable and valid?
7 If a diagnostic test is technically inadequate, is it likely to lead to outcomes which are false positives (indicating a

problem where none exists), false negatives (indicating no problem where one does exist), or both?

8 Are children's sub-test profiles on the WISC-R an un-impeachable source for the differential diagnosis of learning difficulties?

9 Has instruction which is matched to children's modality preferences been accepted by researchers as completely effective?

10 Name one feature of a learning situation which might be related to a child's failure to learn, other than an obtained profile of psychological abilities.

GUIDELINES:

After attempting all ten questions, compare your responses with the answers given for this purpose. An acceptable mastery level for Review Two is eight questions correct. It is suggested that you look through the text related to any incorrect responses. (Page numbers are listed against the answers in the Answer to Reviews section, pages 141–6, to help you do this quickly.) Should you have less than eight answers correct, it is likely that you will profit from re-reading the preceding section for a fuller understanding.

3
Selecting valid programme content

In setting out to build up learning from a foundation of instructional methods, the programme orientation offers a powerful alternative to the ability based approach. One could say that it attempts to work from the outside of the child inwards, rather than the inside of the child outwards. Whatever we want the child to learn, when teaching has been completed, we expect that he or she will afterwards be able to do something which he could not do before. teaching begins, i.e. a causal relationship is implied between *teaching* and overt skill. Gagné (1977) suggested that this called for consideration, firstly, of which competencies should actually be acquired (*What do we teach?*); secondly, what teaching input will support the internal processing required to learn them (*How do we teach it?*) and, thirdly, how superfluous material or activities can be eliminated (*What do we not teach?*).

From such a standpoint it can be seen that instructional procedures need to be carefully organized, and Bloom (1968) suggested that any learning programme setting out to ensure mastery of the content taught would require several basic features (see Fastcheck 9).

Given an instructional emphasis, programmes for special-needs children necessarily grow from selected learning tasks and feature explicit teaching procedures. However, as Stones

Fastcheck 9	**Critical features of learning-for-mastery (LFM) programmes**
	1 Clearly specified objectives.
	2 Small units of learning derived from related sets of objectives.
	3 Valid but short learning tests.
	4 Preset mastery levels for learner performance.
	5 Clear communication regarding what and how to learn.
	6 Corrective provision for learners who fail on a mastery test.
	7 Monitoring all learners through to mastery.

(After Bloom, 1968)

(1983) has indicated, while there is a fairly substantial body of knowledge about human learning, there has to date been a lack of systematic attempts to apply this knowledge to teaching, the emphasis in teacher-training institutions having been on theory *per se*, rather than its application to the classroom situation. Of course, exposure to educational theories is not in itself a sufficient condition for the design of effective learning programmes and a more radical view might question whether it is even a necessary condition. What most certainly is needed is a methodology which applies what is known about the psychology of the learning process to instructional procedures.

A practical solution for teachers was described by Engelmann (1977):

> There is no magic to instruction. If the instruction is carefully designed, if the demonstrations are consistent with only one interpretation, if the operations are initially overt and perfectly clear, if the pre-skills are identified and taught (without teaching other skills that 'may be' important) you will succeed. Remember, don't start by observing the child. Start with the task.

This is not to say that one should avoid looking at the child, but rather that it is preferable to view him in relation to the actual task to be mastered. Analysis of the task cannot be taken as the whole story, since the task itself is just one component of the interaction involved in producing a given learning outcome, albeit one which helps to determine how to shape the teaching presentation.

In order to develop a particular programme, it is clearly necessary to have some guidelines to apply, and these will form the subject matter for the sections which follow. It should be understood from the outset that this orientation is didactic, i.e. it works from a given concept or rule which is outlined by positive and negative examples in order to reduce initial demands on the learner. As such, it is diametrically opposed to a 'discovery' approach, which makes the learner responsible for finding out the rule for himself. Of some importance here is Ansubel's (1968) review of the research literature on discovery learning which concluded that most of the reasonably well-controlled studies reported unfavourable outcomes. On the other hand most studies citing positive findings had either failed to control important variables or employed questionable techniques of statistical analysis.

If children with special needs were able to learn effectively on their own in school, or learn appropriate coping strategies from normal class teaching, presumably their learning difficulties would have evaporated without further intervention, and their learning performance would have been indistinguishable from that of their 'normal' peers. It must be assumed that all children capable of perception are able to learn, but for a teacher the safest assumption will be that more learning will come from adult goal-setting and supervision.

Since it is impossible to attempt all known educational goals simultaneously, those we select at any one time must lead us to discard others and thereby influence programme content to a very marked extent. A parallel may be found in the selection of geographical goals, in that if we decide to travel, say, to a given northern city from a current southern location, it is very likely that we will pass through other known centres of population *en route*, thus creating a fairly predictable journey. Although it may seem to be putting the cart before the horse, in fact the chosen goal represents a starting-point in the design process. While a goal may, of course, be outlined in terms of some required teaching activity, in the long run it is probably more productive to phrase it initially in terms of pupil performance, and then use this information to plan the teaching input most likely to produce the outcome desired. At this stage of the planning process a number of questions can be asked so as to refine a programme and the following are among those which it will be useful for you to consider:

1 *What is the essential goal for the curriculum component with which you are concerned?*
   (Could the children possibly succeed in this area of their work without it?) In other words, the essential goal probably represents at least a *minimum* acceptable level of performance, and as such should be in accord with the expectations of colleagues who may have responsibility for teaching the same children at a later stage. Ideally then, the goal will be a forward-looking one, which will help children to cope with the more complex demands they will meet at a higher level of the curriculum later on.

2 *Is the goal stated in terms of pupil performance?*
   (Does it state just what the child should be able to do?) Implicit in this is the idea of creating maximum clarity *vis-à-vis* the outcome. Therefore, while it is important to have a description of just *what* will be done (the *instructional* objective), it is equally important to be clear about *how well* it should be done (the *performance* objective), to know when mastery has been achieved. It can be seen in this regard that the objective 'write your name' is one thing; 'print your name clearly with all letters the same size and each one touching the line' is obviously a more rigorous objective.

3 *What skills are critical for realization of the goal?*
   (Would that same outcome necessarily be impossible without them?) Having set the goal, it is likely to be more efficient if we allow as little variation in the range of skills required as is humanly possible. For every new type of skill we introduce, the probability increases that some of them may not be critical in the achievement of the goal intended. If you wanted children to reach the goal of telling the time to the nearest minute, there would be little point in working on skills like identifying several different kinds of clock, for instance. Given that goal, such an activity could be a waste of time!

4 *Is the goal as it stands likely to make equivalent demands on both boys and girls?*
(Is it an equal opportunity goal?) If the answer to this question is 'no', because of existing differences you have observed in the skill-profiles of boys against those of girls in your group, then to be sure that they will all attain the goal, you will need to even out their status before they start to work towards the goal intended. Say that your goal was to have each child change a fuse for an electrical appliance within five minutes, this might well discriminate against girls if they had, in general, received less practice at manipulating a screwdriver, the key implement involved. Here, it could prove useful to provide an initial booster experience for any girls who were not proficient enough at the outset.

From this it can follow naturally that we next consider the programme content through which the goal may be approached, and which relates very specifically to that goal in order to minimize the learning time involved. Since the goal established will require a certain type of performance from the child, it also follows that the intermediate objectives will make distinctive demands upon him. If an appropriate goal is to catch the 8.15 a.m. local bus to school, this might suggest intermediate objectives such as being completely dressed forty-five minutes earlier, finishing breakfast fifteen minutes earlier, leaving home ten minutes earlier and reaching the bus stop five minutes earlier than the bus departure time. Each of these objectives calls for its own set of performance skills to produce dressing, eating, locomotion and queuing, etc., as required. For the teacher, those rules and actions the child must learn in order to match his performance to the objectives will help to determine what has to be taught and what material can be safely left out.

The purpose of having a defined goal and objectives is conveyed by the words of a popular wall poster which says, 'if you don't know where you are going you might end up somewhere else.' The implications of using an objectives approach were described in some detail by Ainscow and Tweddle (1979), the thrust of their argument being that it helps to make instruction more effective. (Kiernan (1981) has shown how this approach can be applied to work with multiply handicapped children.) Hence the selection of what will be taught is a primary consideration in getting a learning programme together, and Engelmann and Carnine (1982), in what is perhaps the most searching analysis of cognitive instruction yet available, provided five useful guidelines for the development of functional programme content:

1 *The items taught should include only those required for the final competency.*
   For example: A reading programme must include decoding skills, but does not have to train children in the discrimination of geometric shapes. A bicycle safety programme must include riding and maintenance skills; it does not need to cover the history of bicycle engineering.

2 *An item should only be included when foundation skills have already been taught.*
   For example: Writing answers to comprehension questions should only follow after decoding and writing competencies have already been established, for to do otherwise might handicap the learner by demanding skills he does not possess. A social skills programme involving payment for goods or services and checking change received, would be appropriate only after relevant coin-recognition and computation skills have been covered.

3 *Each item should possess maximum utility.*
   For example: A reading programme which initially teaches letter-sounds from which decoding may commence, offers more useful information to a child beginning reading than one which teaches letter names from which he cannot decode. A library-skills programme would need to cover alphabetical and numerical coding of subject and authors but would not need to review great works of English literature.

4 *An item should be included only when the learner has achieved mastery (i.e. 80–100 per cent accuracy) on preceding items.*
   For example: Decoding of multi-syllable words could begin when mono-syllabic and bi-syllabic words have been mastered. To start on multi-syllable words could be to enter the programme at the child's frustration level. Likewise, if a

child is only 50 per cent accurate on subtraction of single digits, a shift to subtraction of two digits is not justified.

5 *Any item on which the learner has previously made persistent errors would also need to be included*, as this illuminates what the child needs to learn. (An error might be classed as persisting when it occurs over three consecutive presentations of the same task.)

For example: Over three days running a child answers written maths problems wrongly because he reads 'the' for 'three' and cannot read 'eight'; so his teacher schedules further work on these items. To overlook this difficulty would result in an increased proportion of errors when two and three digit numbers were encountered later in the sequence. In a spelling test, 13-year-old Michael consistently misses out double consonants before an 'ing' ending, so that he writes 'swiming', 'siting' and 'faling'. A review of the appropriate rule and its applications is therefore needed to help him.

Fastcheck 10

Valid content
Valid programme content may include: 1 Material for which there has been adequate preparation. 2 Material which is critical to performance of the goal. 3 Material which overcomes previous mistakes. 4 Material which is relevant and useful for the learner.

In so far as the items taught are derived from the goals selected, it is also important to ensure that the most useful goals are chosen to make optimum use of the time available. The reason is simply that children spend only a finite number of hours in class and special-needs children are not necessarily assigned a longer school day. At approximately five hours a day, for a maximum of 200 school days, the total time in school will be no more than 1000 hours per year.

If this total is to be apportioned to provide for the development of language skills, social skills, motor skills, reading skills, number skills, writing skills, spelling skills, life skills, creative skills and now computer skills, then clearly the amount of time for each will be limited. When one adds to this the recognition that, for a given child, actual time under instruction often represents only a fraction of the total time spent in the classroom, it becomes apparent that there is a great need to use instructional time as productively as possible. Hence the need for careful selection of the content to be taught for, as Swann (1983) suggested, we need to keep in mind the end towards which we are working, and this may require a willingness to recognize that curriculum modifications are needed just as much as any change on the part of the child.

Review three

DIRECTIONS:

To check the extent of your understanding at this point, it is recommended that you attempt to answer all ten questions in the review *before* you look up any of the answers supplied. All of the questions are derived from the text, but you may find some a little harder than others, so do not be surprised if you are unable to answer them all at first; just try your best with each one. You are specifically advised against reading later sections of the text until you have completed this review.

REVIEW QUESTIONS:

1 Does the programme orientation emphasize discovery of rules by the child, or demonstration of rules by the teacher?
2 Would a programme design usually stem from a curriculum activity or from a target child?
3 How can a goal be expressed in terms of pupil performance?
4 Would a highly valid programme include material which was not directly related to the final goal?
5 Should the programme content incorporate completely new tasks without teaching prerequisite skills?
6 Should an item be included if the child has not mastered the prerequisite skills?

7 Should one include items on which the learner has previously made some mistakes?
8 Would the content of a programme normally be derived from the response profile of an individual child on a normative test?
9 Does the approach described focus on implicit or explicit changes in the child?
10 Does the programme orientation derive from a commitment to psychological processes, discovery learning on the part of the child, or principles of instruction?

GUIDELINES:

After attempting all ten questions, compare your responses with the answers given for this purpose. An acceptable mastery level for Review Three is eight answers correct. It is suggested that you look through the text related to any incorrect responses. (Page numbers are listed against the answers in the Answers to Reviews section, pages 141–6, to help you do this quickly.) If you have less than eight answers correct, it is likely that you will profit from re-reading the preceding section for a fuller understanding.

4

Sequencing the programme material

Sequencing programme activities

In learning situations, as in card games, some sequences are more advantageous than others, and one major purpose of providing a series, or sequence, of steps towards a curriculum-based competency is to promote transfer of learning between the objectives involved (Gardner and Tweddle, 1979), as this will accelerate progress. Klausmeier and Goodwin (1975) counselled that the initial item covered should be set at an easy level so that the child could gain success at the first attempt, and Engelmann and Carnine (1982) concurred, with the proviso that the earliest items in a sequence should be drawn from relevant material that the child has already mastered.

Beyond this starting-point, the steps in any special-needs programme should be small enough to allow optimum transfer of learning. Such transfer will logically occur where consecutive steps have the closest possible similarity. Optimum transfer can be expected where the maximum possible number of features are common to the steps involved, so that the learning situations, the tasks involved and the responses called for reflect a high degree of similarity. In situations where the tasks involved differ markedly, the presentations are inconsistent, and different responses are required, transfer of learning is unlikely. If one considers two consecutive tasks in a programme (Task A and Task B), greatest transfer will occur when performance of Task A includes the majority of competencies called for in Task B.

Take, for example, two consecutive items – Item (X) and Item (Y) – in a life-skills programme involving shopping in a supermarket.

Item (X)	Find the lowest priced ½-kilo pack of butter and put it in your basket.

Item (Y)	Find the lowest priced ½-kilo pack of margarine and put it in your basket.

The two tasks involve just one location in the store (dairy products), similar tasks, similar instructions, similar product presentations, and matching responses. Transfer from Item (X) to Item (Y) might therefore be reasonably expected.

On the other hand, should the two items be constructed differently (Item (U) and Item (V)) the implications for transfer are quite different. In this case the complexity of Item (V) is greater than Item (U). It involves a different measurement parameter (kilograms), harder product discrimination, and a second display area (baking products) would have to be located. As this latter feature would not necessarily be near by, it is not the least demanding element in Item (V). Transfer from the first to the second item in this pair would be uncertain, even improbable for some special-needs children.

Item (U)	Find the lowest priced 1-litre carton of milk and put it in your basket.

Item (V)	Find the lowest priced 1.5-kilo pack of self-raising flour and put it in your basket.

Given a longer sequence, the issue of transfer must go beyond the similarity of just two consecutive items. In the writing sequence shown in Figure 2 (see pages 42–3) similarity is reflected not only between items *within* each step, but also *across* the steps themselves. For example, it can be seen that the first three items *within* STEP 1 are very similar indeed, but additionally, the whole skill sequence for STEP 1 is repeated *across* STEPS that follow. When a child can manage, say, the whole of STEP 2 correctly, it is a fair assumption that this will enable him to produce most of the skills demanded for STEP 3. So while this is not the only conceivable sequence which could be constructed, it does appear to incorporate a modest transfer facility.

In constructing programmes with graded sequences such as these, we also need to be aware, as White (1973) pointed out, that every single item in such a sequence may not be essential for every child, and therefore allow that alternative sequences could probably be compiled. Indeed, Bender, Valletutti and Bender (1976) proposed a format (Fastcheck 11) which suggested that a different sequence could be developed for the task of writing one's name.

Fastcheck 11	**An alternative name-writing sequence**
	1 Trace capital letters. 2 Write capital letters without model. 3 Trace small letters. 4 Write small letters without model. 5 Print first name from model. 6 Write missing letters into first-name model sequence. 7 Print last name from model. 8 Write missing letters into last-name model sequence

(After Bender *et al.*, 1976)

A quick look suggests that this sequence, although shorter, may be incomplete for some learners, as it does not provide for separate practice on the component parts of individual letters, and neither is it clear whether transfer to accurate writing of the full-name letter sequence should be expected from separate practice of first and last names. The important question here is whether sufficient transfer is provided for special-needs children and this would probably have to be resolved by a practical test of the sequence shown. This indeed is a vital point, in that no matter how good a sequence looks on paper, it is only as good as the performance it produces in practice. By trying out programme sequences in a live teaching situation, we can discover the different effects of each step on the learner in a way that no amount of speculation or prediction can match.

Actually, step-size can be controlled empirically, if so desired, on the basis of Engelmann's (1977) assertion that learning becomes 'lumpy' when the child's level of accuracy falls below 70 per cent. This offers a possible rule for identifying any difficult or unproductive items in the learning sequence – particularly when several children fail to meet the 70 per cent threshold. From the point of view of transfer, Houghton (1980) provided evidence that, although they take a little longer to develop, high levels of accuracy exercise significantly longer-lasting effects on learning performance. To become highly accurate, however, a learner's errors must be overcome as early as possible, and much practice will probably be needed in order to master the skills involved, for mastery also implies that the rate of responding will be relatively rapid compared with baseline performance. Good and Brophy (1984) concluded from recent classroom research that teachers who set success rates of 90 to 100 per cent tended to produce more learning than teachers who accepted high failure rates.

On new tasks, practice sessions need to be repeated closely together (this is sometimes termed *massed* practice) or mastery is unlikely to be developed. Once this has been attained, however, the relevant skills can be maintained by rehearsals that are more widely separated in time (also known as *distributed* practice). In keeping with the notion of developing mastery, Carnine and Silbert (1979) advised that a change in emphasis, incorporating a shift away from early dependence on the teacher towards later independence on the part of the child, should be developed.

There are other important factors to be considered in compiling sequences for special programmes. Johnson and Morasky (1980) took the view that *Identification* responses

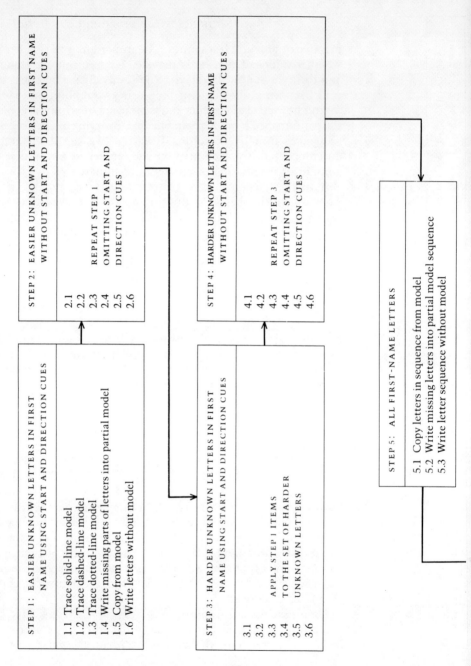

STEP 1: EASIER UNKNOWN LETTERS IN FIRST
NAME USING START AND DIRECTION CUES

1.1 Trace solid-line model
1.2 Trace dashed-line model
1.3 Trace dotted-line model
1.4 Write missing parts of letters into partial model
1.5 Copy from model
1.6 Write letters without model

STEP 2: EASIER UNKNOWN LETTERS IN FIRST NAME
WITHOUT START AND DIRECTION CUES

2.1
2.2
2.3   REPEAT STEP 1
2.4   OMITTING START AND
2.5   DIRECTION CUES
2.6

STEP 3: HARDER UNKNOWN LETTERS IN FIRST
NAME USING START AND DIRECTION CUES

3.1
3.2
3.3   APPLY STEP 1 ITEMS
3.4   TO THE SET OF HARDER
3.5   UNKNOWN LETTERS
3.6

STEP 4: HARDER UNKNOWN LETTERS IN FIRST NAME
WITHOUT START AND DIRECTION CUES

4.1
4.2
4.3   REPEAT STEP 3
4.4   OMITTING START AND
4.5   DIRECTION CUES
4.6

STEP 5: ALL FIRST-NAME LETTERS

5.1 Copy letters in sequence from model
5.2 Write missing letters into partial model sequence
5.3 Write letter sequence without model

STEP 6: EASIER UNKNOWN LETTERS IN LAST NAME
USING START AND DIRECTION CUES

6.1 Trace solid-line model
6.2 Trace dashed-line model
6.3 Trace dotted-line model
6.4 Write missing parts of letters into partial model
6.5 Copy from model
6.6 Write whole letters without model

STEP 7: EASIER UNKNOWN LETTERS IN LAST NAME
WITHOUT START AND DIRECTION CUES

7.1
7.2
7.3   REPEAT STEP 6
7.4   OMITTING START AND
7.5   DIRECTION CUES
7.6

STEP 8: HARDER UNKNOWN LETTERS IN LAST NAME
USING START AND DIRECTION CUES

8.1
8.2
8.3   APPLY STEP 6 ITEMS
8.4   TO THE SET OF HARDER
8.5   UNKNOWN LETTERS
8.6

STEP 9: HARDER UNKNOWN LETTERS IN LAST NAME
WITHOUT START AND DIRECTION CUES

9.1
9.2
9.3   REPEAT STEP 8
9.4   OMITTING START AND
9.5   DIRECTION CUES
9.6

STEP 10: ALL LAST NAME LETTERS

10.1 Copy letters in sequence from model
10.2 Write missing letters into partial model sequence
10.3 Write letter sequence without model

STEP 11: ALL FIRST AND LAST NAME LETTERS

11.1 Write missing letters into partial model sequence
11.2 Write full letter sequence without model
11.3 Extend to worksheets, books, pictures, etc.

Figure 2. One possible instructional sequence to help a child write his name
NOTE: Harder letters might include 's' and any involving a diagonal line; easier letters
would then be the remainder.

43

Fastcheck 12	Programme sequences
	1 Carefully planned learning sequences facilitate the transfer of learning. 2 Transfer of learning is a function of similarity between programme items. 3 Markedly dissimilar items may eliminate transfer of learning. 4 It is unlikely that there is only one perfect sequence for a given task. 5 The effectiveness of a sequence is revealed by the extent to which it leads to changes in the learner's performance.

need to be taught before *Production* responses. After all, if a child cannot recognize something, how can he or she reasonably be expected to produce it? When one says to a child, 'write today's date at the top of your work', it is assumed that he knows what the date actually is.

Johnson and Morasky's definition of *Identification* and *Production* is as follows:

> Before learning to 'produce' the correct response for a given task, the child must learn to 'identify' the correct response. The difference between a 'production' and an 'identification' response is that in the former the child recalls or generates the response from memory, whereas in the latter the child selects the correct response from given alternatives.

From this definition it can be seen that *Identification* would involve a process of *recognition* followed by a relatively small amount of output, whereas *Production* would involve a *recall* process followed by a relatively large amount of output from the child. (In addition, it should be noted that *Identification* also implies some skill in discrimination.)

Perhaps the easiest way to conceptualize the differences between *Identification* and *Production* responses is to think of an input–output system for which *Identification* represents an emphasis on the input side and *Production* represents an emphasis on the output side. (This is an oversimplification, of course, but it serves as an analogy if this limitation is understood.) From an instructional viewpoint, it is not too difficult to train in either kind of response. Both types of response are almost second nature to experienced teachers, and teaching them is a task performed frequently across the course of a typical school day.

The teaching of *Identification* responses is often undertaken as a pair-associate learning task, i.e. a task in which an item and a relevant label are presented together, as when you point out some footwear and say 'shoes', stand up and say your name, indicate a tariff card in a restaurant and say, 'This is the menu', or direct children's attention to the name of a store and say 'Here is Woolworths', for instance.

In Fastcheck 13, you will see an elementary sequence written by the author in 1977 for developing children's recognition of irregular words with which they were encountering particular difficulty. Note that it represents an *Identification* task and, as you read it through, look out for the paired association of item and label early in the sequence and for the discrimination implicit towards the end.

Fastcheck 13	**A sequence for recognizing irregular words**

METHOD:

1 The procedure centres on the use of daily training, backed by tests given at increasing intervals, and the use of progress charts.

2 Give the child daily practice sessions of not more than fifteen minutes in which you have him say on demand the selected words written on small cards.

3 After demonstrating what to do (several times if necessary) give the child ten attempts, during which you provide the correct response each time he makes an error.

4 Assume that a target word is learned when the child can make not less than nine consecutive correct responses out of ten.

5 Reward him *immediately* he achieves 90 per cent accuracy (e.g. with a smile, cuddle, verbal praise, a sweet, or any combination of these).
6 Re-test at intervals of one day, three days, and seven days. If he falls below 90 per cent accuracy on any of these re-tests, begin the whole cycle again. Completion of the learning cycle comes at 90 per cent accuracy on the seven-day test.
7 Keep all words to black-on-white presentation to parallel what will generally be found in books. Use cards of identical size and write in lower-case letters except where the word has an initial capital in the reading book, in which case write and teach both forms.

SEQUENCE FOR TRAINING:
1 Select the word to be learned.
2 Show the child and say the word not less than three times (more if you would like to).
3 Say, 'What is it?' and look at him as though you expect a reply.
4 Say, 'Tell me again', looking expectant.
5 Say, 'Tell me once more', again looking expectant.
6 Praise the child when he is correct.
7 Put the target word with *one* other on a table in front of the child. Point to it, and repeat items 3 to 6.
8 Change the card positions and repeat items 3 to 6.
9 Place the target word with *two* other word-cards and repeat items 3 to 6.
10 Change the positions of all three words and repeat items 3 to 6.

More will be said on the topic of *Identification* later in the text, but at this point, the issue of concern is how to help an unsophisticated learner to develop from simple *Identification* to more complex *Production* activities.

One supportive cue will, of course, be the type of communication employed and different verbal directions might naturally be expected to result in different outcomes regarding the child's performance, as suggested by the statements in Fastcheck 14.

Fastcheck 14

Brief sample statements	
FOR IDENTIFICATION RESPONSES	FOR PRODUCTION RESPONSES
1 Point to . . . . 2 Put your finger on . . . . 3 Show me another one just like this . . . . 4 What is this called?	1 Give me . . . . 2 Draw a . . . . 3 Write this down . . . . 4 Go to . . . .

At this point it will be helpful if you refer to page 66 and read the wording suggested in STEP 2 and STEP 3, noticing how the authors made *Identification* and *Production* responses follow from the verbal model they gave in STEP 1.

Of course, the actual language used represents only one kind of shaping process. Generally speaking, some type of modelling behaviour will also be useful; however, the combined effect of verbal labels and modelling procedures exercises a more powerful influence on shifting the learner from *Identification* to *Production*. If you visualize showing a child a picture of a man with one leg out in front of the other, and saying 'This is *walking*', and then saying the same thing while performing the relevant actions, it should be apparent that the second presentation (which includes a˙ live model) offers the learner more complete information.

A third feature of helping children develop towards *Production* responses is to provide most cues early on in a sequence and gradually reduce the amount of support given as the sequence unfolds. This will help learning to progress more smoothly than it would if the child is thrown in at the deep end of any new task. Examination of the outline on constructing sets by colour, shown in Fastcheck 15, will reveal a more detailed sequence than the one shown for irregular words (see page 48). In considering the 'sets' sequence, bear in mind that the critical

Fastcheck 15

Part of a sequence for shifting the learner from identification responses to production responses when introducing work on sets

DIRECTIONS
Words written in capital letters are spoken by teacher, underlined words being emphasized. Lower-case material is for information.
Have a mixed display of coloured shapes at hand. At this level, colour identification and serial counting skills are assumed.

PRESENTATION

1 'YOU ARE GOING TO LEARN TO MAKE SETS BY COLOUR. WATCH ME AND LISTEN.' (Select a red shape and hold it up.) 'THIS ONE IS <u>RED</u> SO WE PUT IT IN THE <u>RED</u> SET'. (Place item chosen in container, then choose a different red shape, holding it up.)

2 'THIS ONE IS <u>RED</u> SO WE PUT IT IN THE <u>RED</u> SET'. (Put it in, then hold up another red shape.)

3 'THIS ONE IS <u>RED</u> SO WHAT DO WE DO?' *Child: 'Put it in the red set.'* (Put it in.) 'RIGHT, IT GOES IN THE RED SET'. (Then choose a blue shape and hold it up.)

4 'THIS ONE IS <u>NOT RED</u> SO WE PUT IT BACK'. (Put it back and hold up a red shape.)

5 'THIS ONE IS <u>RED</u> SO WHAT DO WE DO?' *Child: 'Put it in the red set.'* (Put it in.) 'RIGHT, IT GOES IN THE RED SET'. (Then choose a green shape and hold it up.)

6 'THIS ONE IS <u>NOT RED</u> SO WE PUT IT BACK'. (Put it back and hold up a yellow shape).

7 'THIS ONE IS <u>NOT RED</u> SO WHAT DO WE DO?' *Child: 'Put it back.'* (Put it back.) 'RIGHT, IT GOES BACK'.

8 'YOUR GO'. (Hold up red shape.) 'THIS ONE IS RED SO <u>YOU</u> PUT IT IN THE RED SET NOW'. (Give it to the child and have him place it correctly.) 'GOOD. YOU PUT IT IN THE RED SET. WHICH SET DID YOU PUT IT IN?'*Child: 'The red set.'*

9 'AGAIN.' (Hold up a different red shape.) 'THIS ONE IS RED SO WHAT DO YOU DO?' *Child: 'Put it in the red set'.* 'RIGHT. DO IT NOW'. *(Continue in the same manner as follows below.)*

10 'THIS ONE IS <u>NOT RED</u> SO WHAT DO YOU DO?' *Child: 'Put it back.'* 'RIGHT, DO IT NOW'.

11 'THIS ONE IS <u>RED</u> SO WHAT DO YOU DO?' *Child: 'Put it in the red set'.* 'RIGHT. DO IT NOW'.

12 'THIS ONE IS <u>NOT RED</u> SO WHAT DO YOU DO?' *Child: 'Put it back'.* 'RIGHT, DO IT NOW'.

13 'NOW PUT IN <u>THREE MORE</u> RED SHAPES BY YOURSELF'. *Child complies.* 'YOU FINISHED THE RED SET. WELL DONE!'

14 (Mix all the shapes together.) 'NOW MAKE A RED SET WITH SEVEN SHAPES BY YOURSELF'. (Child complies.) 'GOOD. YOU MADE A RED SET YOURSELF'.

variable is *colour*, and that the objective is to get the child to a point where he can respond correctly by himself. Note that both communication and modelling are variables subject to careful control.

Other parameters needing controlled application were identified by Engelmann and Carnine (1982). They recommended that:

1 *Silent (covert) responses should not be required in a programme until the operations involved have been exhibited by voiced (overt) activity.*
   For example: Silent reading should be called for only when proficient reading aloud has been established; written answers should be required only when the child has already provided accurate answers of the same type verbally.

   Leon and Pepe (1983) taught covert arithmetical skills in five separate stages:
   1.1 Teacher performs the calculation with overt instructions.
   1.2 Teacher and child repeat the same steps together.
   1.3 Child performs the calculation, stating the instructions aloud as he or she goes.
   1.4 Child performs the calculation, whispering the instructions as he or she goes.
   1.5 Child performs the whole calculation covertly.

2 *Examples requiring the* same *operational steps should be presented in the* same *way.*
   For example: A teacher has planned an activity sequence for work on words with a final *st* sound. It is set up to include these seven steps:

   STEP 1: Say whether target word ends in *st* or not.
   STEP 2: In a group of mixed items, circle words with final *st*.
   STEP 3: Write in final *st* on incomplete target words.
   STEP 4: Read the words written (same order).
   STEP 5: Read the words written (random order).
   STEP 6: Write final *st* words on request.
   STEP 7: Complete sentences with final *st* words and read them.

From this it should follow that the *same* activity sequence is employed for the introduction of words with an initial *st* sound, and likewise with words having a medial *st* sound.

3 *Items that are easily confused, especially those with similar-sounding names, should be widely separated in the presentation sequence.*
For example: Sounds like 'b' and 'd' and words like 'meat' and 'meet', 'their' and 'there', or 'bear' and 'bare' would be candidates for separate presentation.

Similarly, it is advisable not to teach two ways of coding the same material at the same time, to reduce the risk of confusion on the part of the learner. Thus, ideally, letter sounds and the alphabetical names of letters would not be taught simultaneously, nor would twelve-hour and twenty-four-hour clock times.

4 *Initial instruction for any one item should be covered on at least two consecutive days, should be followed immediately by extension activities and then reviewed.*
For example: If one were teaching different kinds of hand-tools including these items:

    A. Hammer
    B. Saw
    C. Chisel
    D. Drill

the programme would then have the conformation shown in Figure 3. It should be noted that, while the items in Figure 3 are introduced one at a time, they are then treated cumulatively for practice purposes.

5 *Reviews of up to six items covered should balance knowledge of the programme content and the child's performance.*
For example: It is suggested that the following items be incorporated:

(a) The two least frequently presented.
(b) The two most recently introduced.
(c) The two having the highest frequency of errors.

WORKING DAY	1	2	3	4	5	6	7	8	9	10	11	12
INDUCTION ITEM	A	A		B	B		C	C		D	D	
EXTENSION ITEM	A	A	A	B	B	AB	C	C	ABC	D	D	ABCD
REVIEW ITEM			A			AB			ABC			ABCD

[After Engelmann and Carnine, 1982, p. 115]

Figure 3. Programme conformation for introducing new items to be taught.

Julie Reeves teaches each multiplication table in two halves. When working on the upper half of the seven-times table (from 7×7 through to 12×7) she notices that several children are uncertain of 7×7 and 9×7, and conducts a brief oral review accordingly. As all of the items have been covered an equal number of times, her review includes the following:

$$\left. \begin{array}{l} 7 \times 7 = 49 \\ 9 \times 7 = 63 \end{array} \right\} \text{ The two items which yield most errors}$$

$$\left. \begin{array}{l} 11 \times 7 = 77 \\ 12 \times 7 = 84 \end{array} \right\} \text{ The two most recently introduced items}$$

In a later lesson, she leads the children through the whole upper half of the seven-times table again in the regular sequence, afterwards coupling this with the lower half of the table to complete the sequence.

Over the last few pages we have been characterizing the task of constructing sequences of objectives as one of maximizing transfer between the items involved and we have looked at some of the learning potential to be gained from this activity. Equally, one might like to think of the purpose of forming sequences as that of smoothing out the flow of information, so that it can be more easily digested by the child. Yet whichever way one chooses to look at it, the putting into sequence of programme items remains one of the most important activities to be undertaken in constructing a programme for learners with

52 Designing Special Programmes

special needs, since they are otherwise unlikely to grasp subtle relationships embedded in the material and may mistakenly respond to items that are essentially related as though they were quite different.

Review four

DIRECTIONS

To check the extent of your understanding at this point, it is recommended that you attempt to answer all ten questions in the review *before* you look up any of the answers supplied. All of the questions are derived from the text, but you may find some a little harder than others, so do not be surprised if you are unable to answer them all at first; just try your best with each one. You are specifically advised against reading later sections of the text until you have completed this review.

REVIEW QUESTIONS

1 Is it more appropriate to construct new tasks on the foundation of those already taught, or without regard for previous learning activity?
2 Would the transfer of learning normally be strongest between similar or dissimilar tasks?
3 Which is the best index of effectiveness for any given programme sequence; the type of adult logic applied to the design, or changes in children's performances?
4 Which has the longest-lasting effect upon performance: low, medium or high initial levels of accuracy?
5 When should *Production* responses be taught: before or after *Identification* responses?
6 Should *overt* learning activity precede or follow *covert* activity?
7 From the point of view of consistency, is it desirable to present examples of the same operation in the same way, or in many different ways?
8 Which is likely to be more effective: a presentation which

offers easily confusable items together, or one which teaches them quite separately?

9 Which instructional procedure is likely to have greater influence: introduction alone, or introduction plus subsequent review?

10 Would you expect that the most powerful influence on shaping a child's production responses would come from the communication employed, the modelling procedure used, or a combination of the two?

GUIDELINES

After attempting all ten questions, compare your responses with the answers given for this purpose. An acceptable mastery level for Review Four is nine answers correct. It is suggested that you look through the text related to any incorrect responses. (Page numbers are listed against the answers in the Answers to Reviews section, pages 141–6, to help you do this quickly.) If you have less than eight answers correct, it is likely that you will profit from re-reading the preceding section for a fuller understanding.

5
Contrasting the programme items

Drawing together programme material that is valid for the goal we have set is an important beginning, but of course the items involved will not be of uniform quality, as they will vary in the type and amount of information carried, and the question of how to present these contrasts therefore arises. The topic of how to display information visually has been the subject of Component Display Theory (Merrill *et al.*, 1981), in which a basic assumption is that all cognitive instruction occurs through the modes of either telling or questioning, which can be combined with two instructional elements (generality or instance) to give four primary forms of presentation (generality; generality practice; instance; and instance practice).

It can be seen that a clear blend of wording and illustration combine to provide more useful information, and quite a lot of contemporary teaching materials now make use of pictorial examples to help children develop concepts. In a recent experimental investigation, Hayes and Readence (1983) confirmed that, at least for science-based concepts, where the text related to the illustration transfer of learning was enhanced.

One should be on the alert for any discrepancies between text and illustration, however, such as can be seen in the sewing directions in Figure 4.

Here the learner is placed in doubt as to whether it is correct

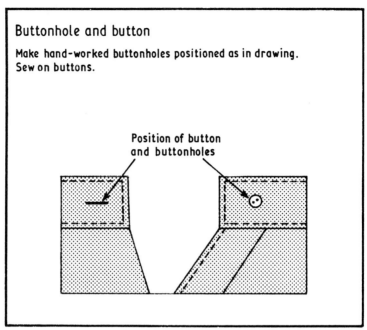

Buttonhole and button

Make hand-worked buttonholes positioned as in drawing.
Sew on buttons.

Figure 4. An example of a picture and text combination not enhancing learning

to follow the picture or to keep to the words instead. As the illustration does not portray quite what the text says, it is difficult to know just how the garment should be finished in this instance.

While the relationship between text and illustration may be important in a general sense for learning, there appears to be at least one important exception, in that it may not hold for learning basic decoding skills in reading. Harzem *et al.* (1976) in their study made children learn to read material which was paired with:

(a) A related picture.
(b) An unrelated picture.
(c) A nonsense picture.
(d) No picture at all.

They found that the poorest learning outcome involved a

Fastcheck 16

Displaying components		
	TELL	QUESTION
GENERALITY	(Describe generality) 'A triangle is a shape with three straight sides.'	(Practice generality) 'What is a triangle?'
INSTANCE	(Display instance) △ 'This is a triangle.'	(Practice instance) 'What do we call this shape?'

(After Merrill *et al.*, 1981)

related picture and the best outcome was derived from the *no picture* condition. It was also noted in this study that *related* pictures had an adverse effect on less able children, i.e. pictures in this category exerted a distracting influence.

Many teachers will recognize that the displaying components model reflects features of their own delivery and it can be helpful to have things described in this way. However, while it may apply in some general sense, children with special needs sometimes need even greater definition. It is still possible that some of them could learn an incorrect rule from the displayed components type of presentation, notably from the triangle example (FASTCHECK 16) that a triangle must always be of a given size and have sides of equal length, which would eliminate many other forms of triangle.

Markle and Tiemann (1970) stated that the minimum number of features to be taught consisted of one positive example, *together with a negative example for each distinguishing attribute*. This injunction is not entirely new, for the juxtaposition of positive and negative examples can also be found in many biblical parables (such as that of one man helping a victim attacked by thieves while another just passed by; or some of the sower's seed falling on fertile ground while some fell on stony ground). However, these authors suggested what seems to be an extension of the biblical technique. In doing so, it appears that they offered a mechanism for achieving a finer degree of discrimination between items in a learning sequence.

> *For example:* A WISDOM tooth is a hammer-like double tooth which is the last to come through the gum at the back of the jaw. It is *not* an INCISOR, a chisel-like tooth which is the first to come through at the front of the jaw. It is *not* a CANINE, which is pointed, single and longer than other teeth. It is *not* a MOLAR, which comes through the gum between the CANINE and WISDOM teeth.

While such a formulation allows for greater definition, Engelmann (1977) more succinctly underlined the essential principle as that of constructing presentations *which would admit of just a single interpretation.* He pointed out that this principle was not trivial, because if a demonstration has more than one interpretation, then some learners will fix on an incorrect one. From this baseline, Engelmann discerned that:

1 *It is impossible to present one positive example of a concept which is consistent with only one interpretation.*
   For example: Holding up a red square and saying, 'This is red' could be taken to indicate that red was the name of (a) a colour; (b) a shape; (c) a movement of the body; (d) a position in space, etc.
   Writing the sign '<' on a blackboard and saying, 'This is less than' might suggest that '<' is (a) of mathematical importance; (b) an incomplete sign; (c) less than a good time; (d) a mouth without a face, etc.

2 *Even a group of positive examples is not necessarily consistent with only one interpretation.*
   For example: If the concept is FURNITURE, then stool, chair, bench, and settee, although positive examples, could allow

some learners to infer that FURNITURE meant only objects to sit on.

If the concept is BIRD, then examples such as robin, sparrow, blackbird, thrush, and finch, might lead some children to think that a bird was (a) only something small; (b) only something that lives near bird-tables; (c) only something that can fly; (d) something which can only be found out of doors, etc.

3 *A set of positive and a set of negative examples must be presented to reveal the limits of the concept and to provide for appropriate generalization.*

For example: A NATURAL DISASTER involves destruction by the forces of nature, like an earthquake, crop failure or storm. It does not involve destruction by human agency or equipment failure, like warfare, suicide, or vehicle accident.

A BOOK is any lengthy work printed on sheets which are bound together – as in a biography, a children's storybook, a volume of Shakespeare or a reference book, etc. It does not include printing in the form of a letter, a card-index, a set of worksheets, or a newspaper.

Note that the primary goal is that of helping the learner to understand a principle which will then allow him to deal with a maximum number of potential applications. It is not to expose him to all known instances and then expect that the principle will somehow become self-evident, as this could require an inordinate amount of time in some cases. The aim is to be utilitarian, constructing material which is gauged to carry a cohesive impact for the greatest possible number of examples, and for which only a very small number of instructional minutes will be involved.

For example: Consider a situation in which it is intended to teach the concept 'Triangle'. The critical dimension is *shape*, and therefore the task is to design a teaching presentation which covers the critical features; namely that a triangle has three sides, the sides are straight, and they meet to form a closed figure with three angles. Also, the range of the concept must be conveyed, since there are several different types, all sharing the same generic label.

Fastcheck 17	Basic design features for the concept 'triangle'	
	POSITIVE EXAMPLES	NEGATIVE EXAMPLES
	1 Examples showing a *right angle* configuration.	1 An *open* figure with three straight sides.
	2 Examples of a *non* right-angle configuration.	2 A closed figure with *more* than three sides.
	3 Examples indicating that attributes other than *shape* do not affect the label.	3 A three-sided closed figure incorporating *curves*.

It can be seen that FASTCHECK 17 offers a specification for delineating the concept 'Triangle' through the use of POSITIVE and NEGATIVE examples. However, although the basic requirements are set out, a means of contrasting the actual examples is not included. Of direct relevance to this point is an intriguing suggestion by Engelmann and Carnine (1982) that once the positive applications have been outlined, discrimination learning will be made more efficient when concept limits are highlighted through *minimal* difference examples. This subtle but sophisticated technique interposes a minimal difference between selected pairs of examples, (one POSITIVE and one NEGATIVE) to provide the learner with information which sharpens the convention involved. Thus he is helped towards a level of discrimination which will eliminate the widest possible range of NEGATIVE examples thereafter, and which potentially includes items which have not been encountered before, as well as those which differ markedly from the POSITIVE items. One possible sequence for a minimal-difference presentation of the concept 'Triangle' is outlined in FASTCHECK 18, and this would follow from an initial descriptive outline such as 'A triangle is a shape with three straight sides', which serves as an advance organizer.

Fastcheck 18

Minimal difference examples for the concept 'triangle'

ITEM PRESENTATION	TYPE OF EXAMPLE	INFERENCE
1 This is a triangle	POSITIVE	A triangle is a closed figure with three straight sides.
2 This is a triangle	POSITIVE	The concept is independent of size.
3 This is a triangle	POSITIVE	The concept is independent of orientation.
4 This is a triangle	POSITIVE	The concept is independent of colouring.
5 This is a triangle	POSITIVE	The concept includes examples where all angles are less than 90°.
6 This is *not* a triangle	NEGATIVE	The concept excludes open figures.
7 This is a triangle	POSITIVE	The concept includes examples with an angle greater than 90°.
8 This is *not* a triangle	NEGATIVE	The concept excludes figures with multiple sides.

9	NEGATIVE	The concept excludes figures with curved sides.
This is *not* a triangle		
10	POSITIVE	The positive attributes (closed figure; three sides) are re-affirmed.
This is a triangle		

There are several features worthy of note in the presentation employed in FASTCHECK 18. Firstly, sufficient examples are portrayed to show that the term 'Triangle' is not restricted to a single type of example. Secondly, the language employed is varied systematically between POSITIVE and NEGATIVE examples to heighten the discrimination between them. Thirdly, the *minimal* difference examples vary by a single attribute; items 5 and 6 differ only in the location of one straight line, and items 9 and 10 differ only in the presence or absence of an angle above the baseline. Fourthly, these minimal difference examples are separated by examples which are *not* minimally different (items 7 and 8).

Having worked out this presentation, the next step is to find a means to check whether the concept is being learned, and for this purpose a set of test-items will be required. Here the idea is to avoid any predictable sequence of POSITIVE and NEGATIVE items, so that the learner is forced to respond on the basis of shape, the critical variable. This avoids the situation of pseudo-mastery, in which a child creates the impression of knowing how to respond correctly, by fortuitously guessing that, for example, alternate items, or maybe every third pair of items are POSITIVE instances of the concept taught.

FASTCHECK 19 provides one solution to this problem, commencing with a POSITIVE item. It is as well to be aware that there are other equally feasible solutions however, not least of which could be to start the sequence with a NEGATIVE item. In a test sequence either option will do, since the aim is to find out whether the learner can vary his responses correctly against POSITIVE and NEGATIVE items and, therefore, which type of example one starts with is not important. Comparison with FASTCHECK 18 (the initial presentation sequence) will also reveal that in order to achieve a simple form of wording, the word order of the presentation ('This is a . . .'/'This is *not* a . . .') has been modified without the addition of new words, to form a recurring question ('Is this a . . .?') applicable to both POSITIVE and NEGATIVE examples.

Fastcheck 19

A controlled-sequence test for the concept 'triangle'			
1	Is this a triangle?	MINIMUM DIFFERENCE PAIR	POSITIVE ITEM
2	Is this a triangle?		NEGATIVE ITEM
3	Is this a triangle?		NEGATIVE ITEM
4	Is this a triangle?		POSITIVE ITEM
5	Is this a triangle?		POSITIVE ITEM
6	Is this a triangle?		POSITIVE ITEM
7	Is this a triangle?		NEGATIVE ITEM
8	Is this a triangle?	MINIMUM DIFFERENCE PAIR	POSITIVE ITEM
9	Is this a triangle?		NEGATIVE ITEM
10	Is this a triangle?		POSITIVE ITEM

With a sequence like that shown in FASTCHECK 19, guesswork would be rendered ineffective as a strategy for identifying POSITIVE examples of a concept. For instance, a learner who predicted that every alternate item was a POSITIVE example would identify just three items (numbers 1, 2 and 5) correctly, by replying 'yes' to items 1 and 5, and 'no' to item 2. Only a child who had truly learned the discrimination would respond with 'yes' or 'no' *appropriately* to all ten items in the test sequence.

Two important points should be understood at this juncture. The obvious one is that the focus of FASTCHECKS 18 and 19 is a *single* discrimination (triangle versus *not* triangle) which limits the cognitive demands made upon the learner and avoids the temptation to teach too much at once. Almost as important, this provides the foundation for all other consolidation and extension activities (e.g. selection, naming, drawing, writing, etc.) which would need to be built into a comprehensive programme about shape.

Quite apart from instances dealing with visual material, with a little ingenuity this mode of presentation can be extended to a number of other applications, some of which may not be self-evident. For instance, in teaching children social skills a popular emphasis is to allocate a considerable amount of time to the development and rehearsal of appropriate sets of behaviour for conversation, shopping, interview performance, etc. Yet while these behavioural functions are wholly necessary, they do not themselves imply understanding, which suggests that there is a place for introducing selected concepts which could support the development of social behaviours. Take, for example, an issue of common concern to parents, which is that children should exhibit good manners in their interactions with others. One way of increasing children's awareness of this issue would be to precede any modelling and practice of the skills involved with an initial introduction to the basic concept, thus providing a mental set for the behavioural processes to follow.

By referring to FASTCHECK 20 at this point, an elementary outline for the concept 'good manners' can be seen, together with a related test. As previously indicated, the early examples cover a range of instances requesting POSITIVE features of the concept, and the eight items employed here include minimal differences between items 3 and 4, and 7 and 8, separated by items which are *not* minimally different. In this case the test sequence differs from the example shown in FASTCHECK 15 by dint of the fact that it starts with a NEGATIVE item, and is twice as long overall. The length of any test is really determined by how far one wishes to go in order to be sure that the learner has a genuine understanding of the concept and, as this standard for acceptance will vary between people, length must be seen as a slightly arbitrary factor. Perhaps the most important element is that the learner should demonstrate accurate understanding on a recurring basis, and therefore enough items must be included to allow for this.

Fastcheck 20

Introducing a social concept by contrasting examples
OUTLINE   You have good manners when you say and do things in the way that is best for other people.
1 You have good manners if you help an old lady to carry home her shopping. 2 You have good manners if you return a pencil that your teacher drops on the floor. 3 You have good manners if you speak to a visitor in your home. 4 You do *not* have good manners if you won't speak to a visitor in your home. 5 You have good manners if you say 'Thank you' when a person gives you something. 6 You have good manners if you usually eat with a knife and fork at mealtimes. 7 You do *not* have good manners if you usually eat with your fingers at mealtimes. 8 You have good manners if you wait until others stop talking before you say something.
TEST PHASE 1 A friend spills orange-juice down his shirt, and you laugh at him. Is that good manners? 2 A friend spills orange-juice down his shirt and you get him a cloth. Is that good manners? 3 You say 'Excuse me' before you pass between two people standing in your way. Is that good manners?

4 You push in front of a lady standing next to the check-out in a supermarket.
Is that good manners?

5 You tread on someone's toe by accident, and then say 'Sorry' to them.
Is that good manners?

6 An uncle sends you a birthday present and you don't bother to thank him.
Is that good manners?

7 Someone asks you what the time is and you tell them to go away.
Is that good manners?

8 A friend of your mother's says 'Hello', and you say 'Hello' back.
Is that good manners?

9 A friend of your mother's says 'Hello', and you say nothing.
Is that good manners?

10 Your teacher asks you if you would like to help tidy up, and you say 'Yes please'.
Is that good manners?

Having looked at the visual and verbal examples presented thus far, you could now be forgiven for concluding that the techniques employed have little relevance if you are accustomed to using three-dimensional objects regularly for teaching purposes. Words and pictures are, after all, only two-dimensional. This would be a mistaken conclusion however, as these procedures for contrasting examples of a concept can be applied to concrete materials with equal effect. It is, of course, important to relate teaching presentations to the world as a whole, not just the needs of the classroom, which if anything underlines the need for instruction which incorporates three-dimensional realities. Some straightforward examples of teaching presentations which include concrete materials have been provided by Carnine and Silbert (1979) and these are displayed in FASTCHECK 21.

Examination of the individual items in FASTCHECK 21 shows that they exemplify the procedures already described (e.g. in the use of a range of POSITIVE and NEGATIVE items, minimal difference examples, and systematically varied language). There is an additional element in this display however, in that the STEP 3 questions increase the level of

Fastcheck 21

Presentations using concrete objects

FORMATS FOR TEACHING VOCABULARY

	OBJECT	ADJECTIVE (colour)	ADVERB	ADJECTIVE (texture)
STEP 1	Teacher models positive and negative examples. Present three to six examples.	'This is a mitten' or 'This is not a mitten' Examples: brown wool mitten brown wool glove red nylon mitten red nylon glove blue sock	'This is orange' or 'This is not orange' Examples: 2 in. red disk 2 in. orange disk 4 × 4 in. orange paper 4 × 4 in. brown paper	'This is writing carefully' or 'This is not writing carefully' Examples: write on board, first neatly then sloppily hand up coat, first carefully then carelessly arrange books, first carelessly then carefully	'This is rough' or 'This is not rough' Examples: red flannel shirt red silk shirt piece of sandpaper piece of paper smooth book cover rough book cover
STEP 2	Teacher tests with yes–no questions. Present positive and negative examples until the students make six consecutive correct responses.	'Is this a mitten?'	'Is this orange?'	'Is this _____ carefully?'	'Is this rough?'
STEP 3	Teacher tests by asking for names. Present examples until students make six consecutive correct responses.	'What is this?' glove mitten sock mitten mitten glove	'what colour is this?' orange brown orange red	'Show me how you _____ carefully' or 'Tell me about how I'm writing' (quickly, slowly, carefully, etc.)	'Find the _____ that is rough.' or 'Tell me about this shirt' (rough, red, pretty, etc.)

After Carnine and Silbert (1979, p. 146)

demand upon the learner by seeking responses in the form of object names, which is an important extra step beyond the 'yes/no' response. It has to be included as the third step here because more knowledge is assumed on the part of the learner, whereas STEP 2 only calls for a single binary choice.

In considering how to contrast programme items, the examples have been deliberately kept simple, in order to highlight the design features involved. With a little thought, you will probably be able to think of other learning situations in which contrast between items is important, and some of those may involve more complex material. Should this be the case, bear in mind that exactly the same principles can be applied no matter what the topic. The aim is to make the essential features of the material distinctive, while reducing as far as possible the amount of information to be processed by the learner, in so far as this is compatible with producing the intended learning outcome.

Review five

DIRECTIONS:

To check the extent of your understanding at this point, it is recommended that you attempt to answer all ten questions in the review *before* you look up any of the answers supplied. All of the questions are derived from the text, but you may find some a little harder than others, so do not be surprised if you are unable to answer them all at first, just try your best with each one. You are specifically advised against reading later sections of the text until you have completed this review.

REVIEW QUESTIONS:

1 Name *one* of the modes, and *one* of the instructional elements in a component display presentation.
2 Is concept formation made sharper by using only positive examples, only negative examples, or juxtaposed positive *and* negative examples?
3 Which would be expected to create fewest learner errors, presentations which favour a single interpretation, or those which are open to several interpretations?

4 Is the presentation of a single positive example consistent with forming a single interpretation?
5 Would the presentation of several positive examples necessarily lead the learner to a single conclusion?
6 Could you lead children to a single conclusion by the combined use of positive and negative examples?
7 Is the rate of learning likely to be improved most when the communication employed is varied systematically between positive and negative examples, or when it varies at random?
8 Does a planned teaching sequence by itself provide evidence that the child has learned what the sequence was planned to teach?
9 What purpose is served by including performance tests in a programme?
10 Which are the *minimum* difference pairs in the following sequence of words? radish, ash, flask, flash, mesh, crush, crust, foremost, mush, much, swish, wash.

GUIDELINES:

After attempting all ten questions, compare your responses with the answers given for this purpose. An acceptable mastery level for Review Five is nine answers correct. It is suggested that you look through the text related to any incorrect responses. (Page numbers are listed against the answers in the Answers to Reviews section, pages 141–6, to help you do this quickly.) If you have less than eight answers correct, it is likely you will profit from re-reading the preceding section for a fuller understanding.

6

Managing learner errors

Observation of a productive adult working on a familiar task will typically reveal an accurate, rapid and smoothly executed performance. On the other hand, children with learning difficulties often make errors in identification (e.g. say 'car' when shown a picture of a bus), discrimination (e.g. transpose names within a range of colours), production (e.g. omit bar from letter 't', or tail from 'y'), sequencing (e.g. writes 91 for 19, or freind for friend), or some combination of these.

We can begin to understand the occurrence of errors once we recognize that it is in part due to the complex nature of most learning tasks. Inevitably, this allows only a narrow range of responses to be termed 'correct', although the child must produce these from a vast range of potential responses, most of which will be inappropriate for the task in hand. It is a simple fact of life that there are numerically many more 'wrong' than 'right' responses available for him or her to use. If we ask him to count by 2s, we do not want counting by 3s, 4s, 7s or any other number; if we request the names of primary colours, only four will count out of the whole spectrum. In short, there is a higher probability of error responses than correct responses if the latter are not already known to the children, a situation typical of new learning tasks, on which we should therefore be particularly alert as teachers.

Inadequately constructed programmes also create learner errors and this is akin to the distinction between 'forced' and 'unforced' errors in tennis. Indeed, it should be apparent that the prevention of errors bears an immediate relationship to how the programme is designed and presented, for it is attention to this kind of detail which helps to make learning programmes more effective.

Prevention, it is said, is better than cure, and a number of points germane to this issue have already been discussed here and in a previous paper by Branwhite and Levey (1982). Nevertheless, it seems worth re-stating that if we expect a child to master a learning task with as few deficiencies as possible, then certain minimal requirements follow (see FASTCHECK 22).

Fastcheck 22

Preventing learner errors
1 The presentation must be limited to valid material. 2 Modelling procedures must accompany each task presented. 3 Shaping procedures must be incorporated into the presentation. 4 A practice sequence must follow the model. 5 A test (not including a model response) must follow the practice sequence. 6 Mistakes shown up by the test must be corrected.

When trying to prevent errors from occurring it may also be helpful to bear in mind the following questions:

1 *From the viewpoint of an unfamiliar teacher, what problems might arise from the programme as it is produced?*
(If the teacher can get it wrong, then you can bet some of the children will!)
2 *From the viewpoint of an unsophisticated learner, what problems might arise from the programme as it stands?*
(There are nearly always some children who will take the wrong meaning if things are at all ambiguous!)

When questions of this kind can be answered by pinpointing

potential sources of learner error within the intended programme, the chief advantage is that many problems can be eliminated before children need experience the negative effects of failure.

Unhappily, the prevention of errors represents an issue which seems to be less than well understood by many producers of educational materials, and design flaws are consequently not difficult to find in available commercial programmes. Take as one example, a wide-ranging remedial programme by Hickey (1977), which purported to be effective for dyslexics, slow learners, and remedial readers at an early level. The author described its content as comprehensive, systematic and cumulative, claiming that it could be adapted to the needs and abilities of learners of all ages. While it is difficult to assess the truth of these claims, given the absence of any comparative data in the teacher's manual, two of the assumptions clearly stated therein may more readily be considered. These were that the learner should take full responsibility for practising without the teacher's presence, and also that he will decide for himself when to move on from one item to another. In the light of some of the recent research on effective teaching practices mentioned in Chapter 1, it thus appears that this programme could be substantially improved by an increased emphasis on teacher-led instruction to minimize the amount of trial-and-error learning likely to be involved.

In some contrast, Savage and Millar (1976) prepared a programme manual which laid stress upon the role of the teacher. In this manual, it is made clear that teachers employing their programme are expected by the authors to provide model responses and to determine the child's rate of progress themselves. Hence it can be seen that the two programmes referred to exemplify quite dissimilar rationales for a teacher to consider and would predictably have rather different effects upon the performance of children with learning difficulties.

Quite apart from the varying emphases resulting from differences in rationale, other quite serious deficiencies can be identified in contemporary learning materials. For instance, a recently published maths programme has superlative artwork, but from start to finish fails to provide any correction procedures to aid the teacher; an alternative remedial reading programme has large print, but expects the learner to answer questions written in words which have not been taught before the comprehension sections occur, so that the child could not reasonably be expected to understand the questions; a contemporary comprehension programme advises teachers to provide model responses only after children have worked alone on text which actually provides them with no directions on how to respond.

The errors children make can be helpful in revealing the reasoning behind them and from the discrepancy between the responses requested and the actual error made, show exactly what needs remedying. Hence, what begins as a problem in learning evolves into a problem of teaching, where recurrent learning errors offer cues to the child that his response needs changing, and cues to the teacher that modification of the programme is needed.

For example, all fifteen children in a secondary-school group who had been taught a survival programme for cyclists later failed two test questions relating to vehicle braking distances. When this was shown up by an item-analysis of the test involved, their teacher decided that the programme component involved was too complex for them to understand, and of questionable value overall. This component was therefore eliminated for subsequent groups of children.

From what many teachers already do, it is clear that the correction of errors involves at least two major elements. Firstly, it gives the learner feedback to help him differentiate between correct and incorrect responses and, secondly, it normally follows this by further practice. In some instances a third component can be observed, when the teacher also models the appropriate response before the child is asked to rehearse it alone. Thus a correction procedure is essentially one that actively guides the child towards accurate performance by the same kind of demonstration and practice routines used in initial teaching. This can be seen in the University of Birmingham's (1983) 'Teaching and Correction Materials' package known as 'Datapac', where it has been consistently applied across a very large number of programme objectives.

While the style of correction outlined in FASTCHECK 23 is fairly economical, in that it provides the learner with what probably amounts to the minimal amount of information

Fastcheck 23

The 'Datapac' correction paradigm on a simple spelling error

BACKGROUND

The child is given an oral presentation of key words to write on a worksheet. In this instance, the worksheet has the initial letter 'r' supplied with a blank line for the missing letters: 'r_____.'

PRESENTATION

TEACHER: 'YOU ARE GOING TO WRITE THE MISSING LETTERS. LISTEN. THE WORD IS *RING*. YOU SAY IT.'

CHILD: 'RUN'

TEACHER: 'LISTEN AGAIN. THE WORD IS *RING*. SAY IT.'

CHILD: 'RING'

TEACHER: 'THE MISSING PART SAYS *ING*. WHAT DOES IT SAY?'

CHILD: '*ING*'

TEACHER: 'ING IS SPELT I-N-G (naming letters). HOW IS IT SPELT?'

CHILD: 'I-N-G'

TEACHER: 'SAY THE FIRST LETTER.'

CHILD: 'I' (letter named)

TEACHER: 'SAY THE NEXT LETTER'

CHILD: 'M'

TEACHER: 'N. SAY IT.'

CHILD: 'N'

TEACHER: 'SAY THE NEXT LETTER'

CHILD: 'G'

TEACHER: 'HOW IS *ING* SPELT?'

CHILD: 'I-N-G' (letters named)

TEACHER: 'NOW WRITE THE MISSING LETTERS FOR *RING*.'

CHILD: (Writes 'ing')

TEACHER: 'GOOD. YOU WROTE THE MISSING LETTERS TO SPELL RING.'

required to shape his response, it also has an obvious short-coming. No rationale for change is included. In other words, the feedback the learner receives after making a mistake does not, within the example shown, convey anything to him about the level at which the error occurred, or why his response needs changing.

A pattern of more extensive feedback, which does attempt to remedy this deficiency, was suggested by Siegel and Crawford (1983) in a procedure which they termed an 'elaborated correction'. These investigators found that discrimination learning in children from special-education classes could be improved by providing them with verbal feedback, including the reasons for success or failure. Thus, when a child incorrectly stated that two objects were the same when in fact they differed, he or she was told that they were not the same, and just what the difference between them was, e.g. 'It looks like yours but it is thick, and yours is thin'. Correct judgements on the child's part were followed by a confirming comment, e.g. 'That's right, they are both small'. An *elaborated* correction-procedure applied to the spelling task in FASTCHECK 23 would therefore produce a slightly revised presentation, such as the one detailed in FASTCHECK 24, and it is suggested that the reader might find it useful to compare the two procedures at this juncture.

From FASTCHECK 24 it can be seen that the corrective feedback varies with the error. When the child makes a mistake in saying the word he is told 'wrong word', but when he is incorrect in saying a letter, he is told 'wrong letter', with the correct response being given each time. Hence an *elaborated* correction provides information to indicate *why* change is needed, and *what* the change should be. On any task where a number of variables have to be processed, this kind of correction would be particularly useful in helping children to control their errors. Take, for example, a matching task where children are required to match shapes of varying characteristics. If, through an *elaborated* correction procedure, errors are responded to with relevant feedback, such as 'wrong shape', 'wrong colour' or 'wrong size' before a correct response is demonstrated by the teacher then their attention is drawn to the most important variable to be controlled.

Fastcheck 24

The elaborated correction applied to a simple spelling error

BACKGROUND

AS FASTCHECK 23

PRESENTATION

TEACHER: 'YOU ARE GOING TO WRITE THE MISSING LETTERS. LISTEN. THE WORD IS *RING*. YOU SAY IT.'

CHILD: 'RUN'

TEACHER: 'WRONG WORD. LISTEN AGAIN. THE WORD IS *RING*. SAY IT.'

CHILD: 'RING'

TEACHER: 'THAT'S RIGHT, *RING*. THE MISSING PART SAYS *ING*. WHAT DOES IT SAY?'

CHILD: '*ING*'

TEACHER: 'THAT'S RIGHT, IT SAYS *ING*'
'*ING* IS SPELT *I-N-G* (naming letters). HOW IS *ING* SPELT?'

CHILD: '*I-N-G*'

TEACHER: 'THAT'S RIGHT, *I-N-G*'
'SAY THE FIRST LETTER.'

CHILD: 'I' (letter named)

TEACHER: 'THAT'S RIGHT, I' (letter named)
'SAY THE NEXT LETTER'

CHILD: 'M'

TEACHER: 'WRONG LETTER. THE LETTER IS N (letter named). YOU SAY IT.'

CHILD: 'N'

TEACHER: 'GOOD, N.'
'SAY THE NEXT LETTER'

CHILD: 'G'

TEACHER: 'RIGHT, G.'
'HOW IS *ING* SPELT?'

CHILD: '*I-N-G*' (letters named correctly)

TEACHER: 'NOW WRITE THE MISSING LETTERS FOR RING.'

CHILD: (Writes 'ing')

TEACHER: 'THAT'S RIGHT, YOU WROTE THE MISSING LETTERS TO SPELL RING.'

Engelmann and Carnine (1982) pointed out that, where attempts to prevent errors arising were mainly logical in character, their subsequent correction would be largely empirical. Correction is typically based on the frequency and type of errors which have occurred and both *systematic* and *non-systematic* errors occur commonly. *Systematic* errors are errors which are consistent, and are present in the work of a child who, for example, given a mixture of add and subtract tasks, adds the numbers in each type of task, the *systematic* error being that he responds to the minus signs as plus ones. *Non-systematic* errors are variable and may be found where a different child, faced with mixed add and subtract tasks, makes some mistakes in each type of calculation, the *non-systematic* errors arising from a lack of proficiency in all tasks involved. In brief, the major difference lies in the number of error-types involved.

A *systematic* error can be corrected in a separate remedial loop which deals solely with the skill-deficiency involved. Once he has mastered this, the child can be returned to the main programme. *Non-systematic* errors, on the other hand, would take a long time to deal with in this manner, a whole series of remedial loops being necessary which might be difficult to integrate with each other and with the main programme. Here, it is probably more economical to step back in the main programme to the point at which the required skills were first introduced, and then work forward. The forward progress would then be a function of the rate at which mastery was achieved, which, given the child's previous exposure to the same material, should be more rapid than during the initial run.

A common experience is to find that children make an occasional mistake as a result of changing demands at different points in a programme and it is, of course, desirable to vary the teaching input accordingly. Some indications of the range of intervention are listed in FASTCHECK 25.

When a child is having particular difficulty, it can be helpful to record any trends observed in his errors by making repeated observations over the same item. It thus becomes possible to find out not only about his progress, but specifically which items cause particular difficulty. This is important, because

Fastcheck 25

Changing the input according to the error

POINT OF FAILURE	TEACHING INTERVENTION
1 FAILURE TO GIVE VERBAL IDENTIFICATION	State the correct response and ask the child to repeat it.
2 FAILURE TO DISCRIMINATE BETWEEN DIFFERING ITEMS	Point to the most significant item, highlight the features which make it different, and then repeat the items.
3 FAILURE TO TRANSFER BETWEEN SIMILAR ITEMS	Point out the identical features, then repeat the items.
4 FAILURE TO MAKE A COMPLETE RESPONSE	Model the whole response. The ask the child to do it with you. Finally, ask the child to do it alone.
5 FAILURE TO WRITE LETTERS OR NUMBERS WITH THE CORRECT ORIENTATION	Provide a written model. Also give start and direction cues. Ask the child to practise until 90 per cent accurate on the error items. Finally, fade the model and cues, from solid through dashed and then dotted lines, to get proficiency at each level, before work without these supporting devices is attempted.
6 FAILURE TO UNDERSTAND THE DIRECTIONS, GIVEN THAT PREVIOUS PERFORMANCE OF THE TASK WAS CORRECT	Show how the current and previous directions mean the same thing.
7 FAILURE TO GIVE A VERBAL RESPONSE WHICH IS KNOWN	Switch to a brief set of simple questions which require one-word answers that the child should give on demand. Once he is responding smartly, transfer back to the learning task and repeat the original question.
8 FAILURE TO GIVE A WRITTEN RESPONSE WHICH IS KNOWN	As for item 7 above, but use a simple motor task such as 'Simon says' or the child writing a short group of numbers or easy words. Transfer back to the original task immediately the alternative activity has been completed promptly.

(After Engelmann and Carnine, 1982, p. 310)

there may quite possibly be subtle individual variations in error responses within the same programme, which could then be highlighted.

Fastcheck 26

Elementary record of errors made

CHILD *MARK WESTON*   INSTRUCTOR *D. Ward*

	PROGRAMME LOG						
	ENTER CALENDAR DATES IN TEST COLUMNS						
WORD	TRAINING SESSION	ONE-DAY TEST	%	THREE-DAY TEST	%	SEVEN-DAY TEST	%
	5 minutes	18-7-80		21-7-80		28-7-80	
another	"	"	60	"	100	"	100
as	"	"	90	"	100	"	100
attack	"	"	90	"	80	"	100
back	"	"	80	"	100	"	100
belt	"	"	60	"	100	"	100
called	"	"	20	"	20	"	20
came	"	"	20	"	100	"	100
corner	"	"	50	"	50	"	100
could	"	"	10	"	10	"	20
cowboy	"	"	30	"	100	"	100
cried	"	"	10	"	100	"	90
dog	"	"	50	"	100	"	100

The record can be quite simple, as can be seen from the example in FASTCHECK 26 which gives data from an 8-year-old boy learning twelve words previously read incorrectly. The aim was to achieve 100 per cent accuracy over ten presentations of each word, and his teacher gave him an initial five minutes' training on flashcard examples, providing him with a verbal model to start with, and correcting his errors thereafter. On the test given after day one, Mark did not reach the target level for any of the items and was set the task of going over them again with another child acting as tutor. At the end of the three-day test he was 100 per cent accurate on eight words, and by the end of the seven-day test, without further help, had attained the standard level on nine items.

At this point he clearly needed help with words having initial 'c' and final 'd', although this was not given on 'cried' since he was already 90 per cent accurate here on the test and could also manage this word in his reading book without difficulty. Accordingly, 'could' and 'called' were separated by an interval of a week for teaching purposes in view of their similarity, and in fact the child did subsequently reach the 100 per cent level on these two words as well. Without the personal record, this individual difficulty might have gone undetected.

More sophisticated skills-based recording techniques have been systematically incorporated into *The Precision Phonics Programme* compiled by Levey *et al.* (1985). In this programme, instruction on the objectives for separate phonic skills is matched to a child's performance profile, in a way which allows for rapid recording of both correct and error responses as the child learns, thus providing a record which is sensitive to quite small fluctuations in the way the individual child may function. For your information, this technique, known as 'Precision Teaching', is more fully described on pages 94–126.

The issue of dealing with errors is one which most teachers have come across many times in the course of their work. Far from being just a sign of incompetence on the part of the child and a nuisance to the hard-working teacher, it should by now be apparent that errors in reality carry some intrinsic value, for their occurrence leads to change. They tell us that the child has passed some particular limit of understanding, so that something needs to be done differently to get back on the track to the goal, much as we correct our course should we wander across the lane-markings while driving along a motorway. Expressed more strongly then, errors should therefore be regarded as an instructive part of the learning process for all of us.

Review six

To check the extent of your understanding at this point, it is recommended that you attempt to answer all ten questions in the review *before* you look up any of the answers supplied. All of the questions are derived from the text, but you may find some a little harder than others, so do not be surprised if you are unable to answer them all at first; just try your best with each one. You are specifically advised against reading later sections of the text until you have completed this review.

REVIEW QUESTIONS

1 Name three types of error often made by children with learning difficulties.
2 Which highlights the need for help: the overlap between response demanded and response given, or the discrepancy between them?
3 Name *one* thing which can be learned from examining recurrent learner errors.
4 Name *two* ways in which corrective feedback compares to initial teaching procedures.
5 Identify *one* way in which *systematic* and *non-systematic* errors differ.
6 If a child writes the digit '1' last, on all numbers from 14 through to 19, is that a *systematic* or a *non-systematic* error?
7 If a child fails to name an item correctly, what is the most economical type of response for the teacher?
8 What is the major difference between a simple and an elaborated correction?
9 When a child makes a discrimination error, what should his or her teacher do?
10 If a learner makes a response which is incomplete, what kind of teacher input will help him or her?

GUIDELINES

After attempting all ten questions, compare your responses with the answers given for this purpose. An acceptable mastery level for Review Six is eight answers correct. It is suggested that you look through the text related to any incorrect responses. (Page numbers are listed against the answers in the Answers to Reviews section, pages 141–6, to help you do this quickly.) If you have less than eight answers correct, it is likely that you will profit from re-reading the preceding section for a fuller understanding.

7

Computer-assisted learning programmes

There is not space here to complete a full treatise on computer-assisted learning (CAL), but brief reference must be made to some of its basic attributes in order to put certain design issues into context. Despite the rapid absorption of British government funding for schools seeking to acquire microcomputers (a recent Council-for-Educational-Technology estimate is that approximately 34,000 machines have been supplied in this way and nearly all special schools are now thought to have at least one microcomputer), and also the widespread dissemination of software through the Microelectronics Education Program, to say nothing of the exponential growth of microtechnology – all relatively recent developments – the use of computers to solve learning difficulties is still in its infancy. Nevertheless, as Rostron and Sewell (1984) described, a wide range of hardware and software applications has already been developed for special-needs children. Although the quality varies considerably, there can be little doubt that events to date signify a great deal of further development in this area, and it is consequently important that we should not underestimate the potential of CAL just because research and development are at an early stage.

Commercial hype aside, a major advantage of computers is that they operate with great consistency, a feature which is in marked contrast to the human agent, for whom variability of performance is a dominant characteristic. Since the need for consistency is a theme often repeated in special-education circles, this attribute alone should be a sufficient recommendation for us to explore the possibilities of CAL. Another positive factor is that computers are not subject to the effects of fatigue or cognitive strain which human instructors do experience with two important side effects – firstly, their performance is likely to deteriorate and, secondly, their awareness of this change may become reduced. Apart from this, computers can give immediate feedback, as they will not be distracted by classroom management problems, nor will they send children away because they are busy with someone else. Moreover, in terms of the information which they process, computers have 100 per cent recall, another quality which contrasts favourably with fallible human memory. Additional advantages are that, within the limits of the school day, computers can provide virtually unlimited amounts of practice, have the capacity to keep a complete record of each child's performance (Behrmann, 1984), and can also modify instructional procedures in relation to individual differences in responding. (The fact that not all programs instruct the computer to do this is more often a shortcoming in design than a problem with the hardware.)

Having said all this, the equation of computer-based instruction also contains another significant value: disadvantages. The chief disadvantage is the difficulty that the average micro-computer can appear unintelligent in human terms! It is only a machine and therefore lacks human perception and sensitivity. It will reproduce presentation flaws over and over again where a teacher would eliminate them. It can function in a most frustrating way for the human operator, by demanding machine-like repetition of responses from someone trying to be spontaneous and creative. Sometimes it will leave undone that which it not only ought to have done, but has done satisfactorily before – presumably because some electronic gremlin produces minute and random fluctuations within the complex circuitry – but of course the lost function will be inexplicably restored after a while. (Typically this will be just after you have invoked the help of someone with vast expertise, who will probably leave you with just the shreds of your sanity as a result!)

Sometimes the micro will fail to grasp what would be blindingly obvious to the most inexperienced teacher – that when a child enters 'io' this is intended to be '10'; that 'ate' is meant to be 'eight', or 'six' to be '6'; or that no difference in meaning is intended by the learner simply because he happens to omit parentheses from his entry, or makes it in lower-case letters rather than capitals. Perhaps it would be constructive to view the classroom micro with its operational rigidity much as we would think of the limited functioning of a child subject to mental deficiency, the best results being achieved under the direction of a skilful teacher!

Of primary interest here, however, is the question of software design, and the way in which we set about tackling it largely depends upon one's personal persuasion. To have been persuaded that computers are akin to the eighth wonder of the world is probably a viewpoint which leads to the broadest possible application of design knowledge specifically to computer courseware. On the other hand, to have been persuaded that the best kind of computer for the classroom is the model operating within the teacher's head probably leads one to examine various modes of instruction, of which CAL is just one. Whatever one's leaning, it is vital to realize that, from the point of view of design, essentially the same considerations are involved, i.e. the criteria for assessing the instructional effectiveness of computer programs are not vastly different from those employed for assessing other forms of presentation. To paraphrase Marshall McLuhan, in this context we need to concentrate on the message and not get beguiled by the medium.

A microcomputer will happily assume that the child's visual, auditory and motor systems are intact, that he is familiar with the keyboard, concept-board, or other input device, and will faithfully convey whatever quality of information has been provided within the loaded program. Therefore, it is towards the design detail of the program that attention needs to be directed if teachers are to avoid a financially ruinous and grossly inefficient situation in which they have to purchase and use every program before its suitability can be assessed. Evaluation will necessarily depend upon what the program sets out to provide, and how each teacher's priorities are defined; however, there is a variety of program types to be aware of, and of these, four of the more commonly encountered ones are outlined in FASTCHECK 27.

Fastcheck 27

Simple classification of computer programs				
TYPE	OPERATION	SAMPLE	DESCRIPTION	PUBLISHER
Drill and practice	Chiefly presents discrimination learning tasks	'Early Reading'	Visual sequencing tasks involving, e.g. recall and construction of words from an array of letters, and of sentences from an array of words	E.S.M., Duke Street, Wisbech, Cambs. PE13 2AE
Tutorial	Provides for individually tailored problem-solving routines	'Eating for Health'	Offers individualized dietary analysis suitable for adolescent children with moderate learning difficulties. For integration into a life-skills curriculum	Hill-MacGibbon, St Bartholomew's House, Fleet Street, London, EC4Y 1DH
Simulation	Teaches cognitive strategies based upon real-world situations	'Bank'	Simulates personal banking services, such as paying in by cheque, or using a cash dispenser	Hill-MacGibbon, St Bartholomew's House, Fleet Street, London, EC4Y 1DH
Learner-directed	Responds to control instructions from the child	'Dart' (A Logo derivative)	Makes a turtle icon move around the VDU screen according to instructions such as 'forward'; 'backward'; 'left'; 'right'; and amount parameter, e.g. 'right 30' or 'forward 25'	E.S.M., Duke Street, Wisbech, Cambs. PE13 2AE

(So-called 'Interactive' programs are not distinguished separately here because all programs call for some degree of interaction.)

Although only four main types of program are referred to in FASTCHECK 27, in practice the situation is complicated by the fact that program compilers sometimes mix the different types of operation within the same program. (While this is not necessarily a bad thing, it can, of course, render attempts at a simple classification invalid!) However, programs might in general be said to range along a control dimension in which varying degrees of freedom are assigned to the learner. One could think of this as a basically developmental model in which a drill-and-practice entry level would allow least freedom of control to the child, but where higher levels of operation would gradually offer more independent control.

Because of the previously referred to need for extensive practice to help in the mastering of skills, it follows that programs with an emphasis on drill and practice will be likely to be of greatest usefulness for helping special-needs children. Although such programs are sometimes criticized by writers in the educational press as tedious, it should also be realized that they can offer a valuable foundation for the development of skills. Once certain discriminations have become learned, it then becomes possible to develop more sophisticated skills – perhaps those of comprehension or analysis – but unless the discrimination capability is established first, there is little hope of subsequently building up higher-level cognitive activities. A final point about drill-and-practice programs is that they can sharpen selected skills relatively quickly, and by incorporating them into the earliest stage of a developmental model of the learning process, we can help children to become competent as rapidly as possible.

From the teacher's point of view, a critical question to ask about any computer program intended for use in overcoming learning difficulties would be *'Is there sufficient instructional content?'* Looked at from a different angle, it is all very well having an adventure-games style of presentation, multi-colour graphics, tonal or vocal feedback, or indeed whole strings of questions, but if the program has actually taught nothing in the first place, all of the other features could be considered a waste of time and money. From the amount of instruction (rather than plain opportunity to explore), other questions follow, such as *'What does it teach?'*, the point being that whatever skills the program teaches should be of meaningful character and worth spending time on. A supplementary question of equal validity would take the form *'How is the content taught?'* Here an already familiar theme would be struck, for one would want to look at whether adequate modelling, practice, correction and recording procedures had been included in the design. As Bell

(1985) suggested, and sampling readily confirms, the development of computer software has proceeded more or less
independently of the knowledge base for instructional psychology, and one is therefore frequently in the position of providing
negative answers to questions like those just asked.

There are a number of other significant features to consider.
Miller (1985) has drawn attention to a possible problem where
the demands of interacting with the program content are less
complex than those required for operating the computer itself,
because the child might never get started. A related issue
concerns any natural-language communications involved in
the program, for if these are embedded without procedures for
checking that the child has mastered the relevant vocabulary,
then parts of the program's content may remain incomprehen-
sible to him or her.

If the program covers a wide range of skills, some attempt
needs to be made for the child to enter at a level compatible
with his existing skills, through the provision of multiple
points of entry. Omission of this facility can make children's
difficulties seem more serious. For instance, a girl known to the
author became frustrated with a program when she discovered
that in order to reach the level of difficulty appropriate to her
needs, she had to work through every item on each of three
lower levels first. This was rather time-consuming and, of
course, her motivation to use the program was soon lost as a
result. A facility to begin at the relevant level of difficulty
directly could have preserved her interest and this could
perhaps have been achieved through the mechanism of an entry
test at the start of the program.

Timing is another important consideration, in terms of how
long a given stimulus item is actually displayed for the learner
to see, and also the duration of time afterwards allowed for the
child to think and respond. Some programs allow relatively
lengthy periods of time to elapse in each case, but of course this
carries the risk that opportunities are created that may
encourage the child to attend to something else altogether, and
may cover little content if the pace is unduly slow. At the other
end of the scale, very short time spans may make it impossible
for some handicapped children to make their response before
the presentation moves on, and so this can be a somewhat

tricky problem because of variations in response time between children in the same teaching group. Its resolution would seem to be in a more sophisticated level of design, which could reduce the risks either by allowing for timing to be controlled by the teacher on the basis of known differences between individuals, or by the computer so that it works on the basis of an initial test which would check the learner's reaction time on representative tasks, and adjust subsequent display and response time accordingly.

Since the child's attention will mainly be directed to a Visual Display Unit (VDU) – the visual interface between himself and the computer program – the way in which information is presented on the VDU is of relevance in promoting effective learning. In a discussion of video-disc-based instruction, Kearsley and Frost (1985) have made some suggestions which also appear to have use in organizing stimuli on a VDU presentation intended for children with learning difficulties (FASTCHECK 28).

Fastcheck 28	**Design factors for VDU teaching**
	1 Avoid overloading the learner with information in any one display
	2 Emphasize graphics rather than text.
	3 Create text which integrates with the visual display elements.
	4 Avoid extreme contrasts.
	5 Employ visual and auditory cues sparingly to heighten key discriminations.
	6 Organize the features of the display to make it as convincing as possible.

(After Kearsley and Frost, 1985)

Certain of the factors listed may appear obvious to experienced teachers. However, the author was recently in a special class where a boy seemed stuck in a program where he had to scan model text presented on the VDU screen, and then distinguish between target letters of differing heights. A simple enough task, but for the fact that the model text was formed of letters in which tops and tails were reduced to match the size of other letters, so that the heights of all letters were virtually identical. Needless to say, the child was rapidly taken off this program. In a second instance, a child was correctly typing in plain English instructions for an animated figure in a learner-directed type of program, but the VDU display was one in which all the words were run together without any spaces, so that they were unreadable to the little girl concerned. When elementary design errors of this kind can be found in existing software, it seems worth taking the risk of stating the obvious – as apparently it is not quite so obvious to at least some software designers.

Next we come to the question of how the designer has made the program respond after the learner has entered his input. If the computer has been instructed to operate a simple '*if – then*' procedure, for example:

'*If* correct, *then* present next item'
'*If* incorrect, *then* repeat previous item'

Behrmann (1984) contended that this routine might not cater sufficiently for individual differences in children's performance, as an indefinite number of repeats may follow from the same incorrect response. Because of the learners' need for corrective feedback to reduce errors (Rouse and Evans (1985), for instance, found that drill-and-practice alone did not provide this), a program is likely to be more effective if at least a minimal change threshold is incorporated, for instance that a third incorrect response on any one item triggers a corrective procedure.

Rostron and Sewell (1984) provided examples of computer corrections following questions posed in a discrimination learning program (FASTCHECK 29).

Apart from these corrections, if a child enters a response which the computer is unable to recognize, the program design is such that the VDU gives a read-out stating, 'I do not understand', and when the child gives an instruction which the program is unable to carry out, it displays 'You can't'. Such procedures clearly reveal a more sophisticated level of design than that implicit in the use of a standard '*if – then*' routine. It could, of course, prove helpful if a design like this could be extended

90 *Designing Special Programmes*

Fastcheck 29

Simple computer corrections		
	DIALOGUE ONE	DIALOGUE TWO
Computer:	'How many squares are there?'	'What is blue?'
Child:	'One diamond.'	'The square.'
Computer:	'I asked about squares.'	'No. The diamond is blue.'

(After Rostron and Sewell, 1984)

slightly to include an elaborated form of feedback, as in
FASTCHECK 30.

There you might have it in mind that DIALOGUE TWO could
have been worded alternatively, as follows:

Computer: 'What is blue?'
Child: 'The square.'
Computer: 'Wrong shape. The diamond is blue.'

This alternative is rather similar, also exemplifying an elaborated
form of feedback; however, the line which provides the
appropriate cognitive set here is the first one, in which the

Fastcheck 30

Elaborated computer corrections		
	DIALOGUE ONE	DIALOGUE TWO
Computer:	'How many squares are there?'	'What is blue?'
Child:	'One diamond.'	'The square.'
Computer:	'Wrong shape. I asked about squares.'	'Wrong colour. The diamond is blue.'

program is asking the child to select by *colour*, and therefore it seems more consistent to maintain the same set in line three of the dialogue where the correction occurs, by referring to colour once again. For this reason the form of feedback shown in DIALOGUE TWO of FASTCHECK 30 is regarded as the correction of first choice.

Another no-less important way in which a CAL program may respond to the learner's input has been described by Ager (1985), who points out that some programs actually include a style of feedback in which more attractive consequences are presented following an incorrect response than come after a correct response. This is recognizable as quite an elementary mistake, as such programs will increase the probability that the child will make even more errors. Understandably, it is not only a superior *quality* of feedback after errors which carries this danger, for the risk may still be present if the *quantity* alone is greater, the point being that either occurs in direct association with error responses. A well-designed program will therefore provide feedback with a relatively high stimulus value (e.g. more colour, sound, and information) immediately after *correct* responses.

By this time, the idea should be emerging in the reader's mind that good software design is certainly not fortuitous! What separates a 'special' from a 'not-so-special' computer program is a great deal of careful planning at the design stage. In so far as this calls for a considerable depth of knowledge about instructional processes, which might well be construed as a mental discipline in its own right, the author is not in favour of the view that teachers in the special-needs sector should be expected to train as computer programmers. A working knowledge of what CAL can offer will, of course, be helpful in professional transactions with computer programmers, but it is primarily in shaping and evaluating the instructional component of computer programs where teachers as a group could more reasonably be expected to develop their existing skills. (On an individual level, certain teachers may naturally develop a vocation for dealing with one or more of the programming languages, however.)

The identification of complex learning difficulties, the monitoring of children's performance, the analysis of educational

2

Designing Special Programmes

tasks and careful curriculum planning are in themselves demanding, and should represent an adequate field of activity for professionals whose speciality rightly exists in a close understanding of how human learning can be developed. It is therefore contended that an expectation that teachers should also be familiar with the Byzantine complexities of writing computer programs represents an unwarranted distraction from their central task, which is essentially pedagogical, and in reality can be managed by no other professional group.

Beyond that, presumably it *is* a teacher's responsibility to determine whether a computer program is adequately backed by support materials, whether there are guidelines for integrating the program into the curriculum, if the program objectives are made clear, if the requirements for monitoring, discussion, or any other form of teacher intervention are specified and if the program content and instructional procedures are up to the task of changing children's performance to meet the objectives stated. As a professional accomplishment, this could become a major contribution towards making computer programs really 'special', and an important part of the total resource management necessary to make a success of computer-assisted learning. We should favour the use of computer programs where they can demonstrably do a job which releases the teacher for more demanding tasks or provide something unique. However, the present state of the science suggests that there is a need to query whether CAL programs are sufficiently well-designed or researched to be unquestionably appropriate or universally effective.

Review seven

DIRECTIONS

To check the extent of your understanding at this point, it is recommended that you attempt to answer all ten questions in the review *before* you look up any of the answers supplied. All of the questions are derived from the text, but you may find some a little harder than others, so do not be surprised if you are unable to answer them all at first; just try your best with each one. You are specifically advised against reading later sections of the text until you have completed this review.

REVIEW QUESTIONS

1 What are some of the main advantages implicit in the way that computers operate?
2 Name two of the disadvantages of using computers which are referred to in the text.
3 Which type of program would be most useful for skills development in special-needs children: drill-and-practice or learner-directed?
4 Give three design features which can improve the content of a CAL program.
5 How could you avoid a child having to work through inappropriate levels of a complex program?
6 How is a child likely to respond if the pace of presentation in a program is too slow?
7 Cite three factors that can improve a VDU presentation.
8 Describe one shortcoming of a simple *if – then* routine.
9 Which design element of a CAL program is the one most likely to reduce learner errors?
10 What would you expect to result from a program which delivered its most attractive consequences following error responses?

GUIDELINES

After attempting all ten questions, compare your responses with the answers given for this purpose. An acceptable mastery level for Review Seven is eight answers correct. It is suggested that you look through the text related to any incorrect responses. (Page numbers are listed against the answers in the Answers to Reviews section, pages 141–6, to help you do this quickly.) If you have less than eight answers correct, it is likely you will profit from re-reading the preceding section for a fuller understanding.

8
Measuring rates of learning

Analysis of changes in children's learning hinges to a large extent on the question of how much they respond correctly. As a given skill is learned, they typically make the correct response more often. There are two major factors which we can apply to measure this change in children's learning performance, namely the measurement of *how accurate* the child is, and *how fast* he is. The *accuracy* factor has a long educational tradition, and is typically encountered either in the form of a score showing the number of items correct against the total number of items given, say 7/10 in a spelling test, or as a percentage figure, say 85 per cent correct over a series of attempts at a given task. *Accuracy* measures are very widely used, and sufficiently familiar to teachers to need no further explanation here. The measurement of *how fast* (the *rate*) is not so widely employed, however, and it is to this that we shall turn our attention, as a valuable design consideration.

To date, the main application for measuring a child's rate of performance seems to have been for physical fitness and athletics skills, but it has considerable potential for programme development, primarily because the speed with which a task is completed offers a time-scaled index of competence on the part of the child. (For example, a child who reads a story correctly and at a rapid rate is usually taken to be more competent than a child who reads the same story accurately but slowly, as the former simultaneously exhibits both accuracy and speed of performance.) Since children with learning difficulties are quite often identified by their teachers as slow to respond, rate measurements can provide important information about the extent to which the children are able to accelerate their learning performance, and therefore seem worth exploring more fully. (A broader rationale has been provided by Branwhite and Becker, 1982.)

The collection of data on children's functioning is not by any means a new development in education, and as a tool for resource management has a parallel in other spheres of human activity. Effectively managed skills development relies in many fields upon the existence of performance-related data, for example in social or management sciences, operational research and numerous training environments. Just as it has aided professionals in other fields, performance data can also help us to manage learning more systematically, and Precision Teaching (P-T) is a method for matching tuition to performance data from the learner. In short, it is a form of data-based instruction and was defined by Kunzelmann *et al.* (1971) as one way to *plan, use,* and *analyse* any teaching style, technique, method, or theoretical position – old or new. Moreover, P-T is about as different from conventional forms of instruction as precision engineering is from clouting one's thumb with a hammer.

The very term 'Precision Teaching' may sound as though a lot of intricate concepts could be involved. In fact, it is based on some very straightforward and by now familiar notions, for example:

(a) that any complex learning task is like a distance race, best undertaken one step at a time, and at a suitable pace;
(b) that performance should change demonstrably with application;
(c) that direct measurement provides a useful index of how much performance changes;
(d) that timing each lap of learning will show up variations in pace in a way that one overall measure cannot, and that the pace established early on will help to determine later performance;
(e) that a picture of events is worth a thousand words.

Whether you are finding out about P-T for the first time, or have previously read something about it, bear in mind that these main ideas underlie the complete precision-teaching technique for evaluating learning.

The application of P-T enables changes in learning to be measured as they occur, and is therefore particularly appropriate for children with special needs or skills deficiencies, or those whose learning potential is in doubt. Since it involves the delineation of learning procedures and regular recording of performance, P-T can identify changes in situations which might otherwise appear static, especially where a child has apparently failed to learn from ordinary group-teaching activities. P-T also offers a new way of taking errors into account on an equal basis with correct responses, and of making specific individual predictions of future performance on chosen skills. Note, therefore, that the suggested application is for *individually tailored* learning programmes, unless you already have access to group data which derive from the programme you are using.

As a model for evaluation, P-T is different because of its continuity and sensitivity to change. The progress of many children has tended, often for reasons of expediency, to be checked at widely spaced intervals of time, which can lead to learning problems going undetected where early intervention might have eliminated them. P-T gives feedback about learning on a day-by-day cycle, so that the teacher has information reflecting up-to-the-minute performance, and this enables any required changes to be instituted promptly.

In order to spell out how you can begin to measure changes in a child's rate of learning, it is intended at this point to turn from a descriptive outline to a concise, step-by-step guide which, as you assimilate it yourself, will help you to develop precision-teaching skills of your own. Each step follows a consistent form of presentation, with specified starting and completion points, a brief outline, a sample application, and a model procedure to work by. If you follow the sequence shown, it should save you a great deal of trial-and-error learning.

This material is presented at foundation level; hence it is assumed that you are not already familiar with precision-teaching techniques, and advanced skills are not presented. Here the emphasis will be on helping you to explore basic P-T procedures, so that you can decide whether to acquire more complex P-T skills later on. Should you already have logged more than ten hours of using P-T, you will find the recommended further reading on pages 154–5 more useful.

Step 1 Pinpoint the task

STARTING POINT When you identify a particular learning task on which the child repeatedly fails.

Outline The key task to select will usually possess two important qualities. In one respect it will be critical for the growth of academic competence, i.e. growth would be blocked without it, and in the other it should be compatible with the learner's existing skills profile. You will already be aware from general monitoring of a child's performance in class that he or she will have an individual profile of strengths and weaknesses in terms of academic skills, and it is strongly suggested that you focus the thrust of your intervention upon what, in your terms, is the child's major skills deficiency. If it is reading, give reading most attention; if writing, intensify the effort applied to writing; if arithmetic, emphasize number skills, etc. The reason for this is twofold: firstly, that curriculum-related skills are then delivered in accordance with the child's greatest educational need and, secondly, that the degree of change created will be closely related to the amount of instruction that the child receives.

COMPLETION POINT When you have defined that single task to which you assign highest priority for the child concerned.

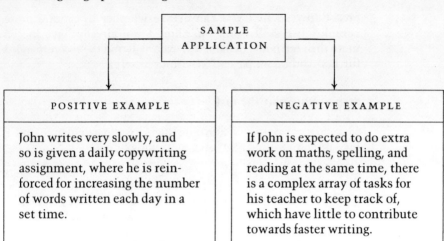

SAMPLE APPLICATION

POSITIVE EXAMPLE	NEGATIVE EXAMPLE
John writes very slowly, and so is given a daily copywriting assignment, where he is reinforced for increasing the number of words written each day in a set time.	If John is expected to do extra work on maths, spelling, and reading at the same time, there is a complex array of tasks for his teacher to keep track of, which have little to contribute towards faster writing.

Fastcheck 31

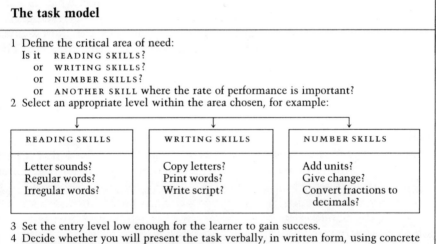

The task model

1 Define the critical area of need:
   Is it   READING SKILLS?
   or   WRITING SKILLS?
   or   NUMBER SKILLS?
   or   ANOTHER SKILL where the rate of performance is important?
2 Select an appropriate level within the area chosen, for example:

READING SKILLS	WRITING SKILLS	NUMBER SKILLS
Letter sounds?	Copy letters?	Add units?
Regular words?	Print words?	Give change?
Irregular words?	Write script?	Convert fractions to decimals?

3 Set the entry level low enough for the learner to gain success.
4 Decide whether you will present the task verbally, in written form, using concrete objects, or with some other form of instruction.
5 Think small. (In P-T small is beautiful!) When you focus on a small task it increases the likelihood that the child will master it quickly and get earlier indications of becoming competent.

FROM HERE GO TO STEP 2

Step 2 Select the learner's response

STARTING POINT When the learner has been identified and the task determined.

Outline A specific response on the chosen task helps you to determine when the learner's proficiency increases. After a failure to learn from ordinary teaching, more structured demands on performance can reduce the range of errors which the child produces. In turn, this can heighten for him the distinction between a correct response and an error response, as there will be fewer alternatives from which to choose. The emphasis should, of course, be on the production of correct responses.

COMPLETION POINT When you have selected the one consistent response which you want the learner to make.

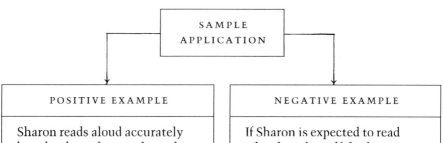

SAMPLE APPLICATION	
POSITIVE EXAMPLE	NEGATIVE EXAMPLE
Sharon reads aloud accurately but slowly, so her teacher asks her to read each page once along with a helper, and a second time by herself with teacher supervision, when her performance is measured. In this way she achieves her optimum reading rate, as she is reinforced for increased fluency.	If Sharon is expected to read silently to herself, look up unknown words in her dictionary, and listen to a tape of an adult reading the same material, many different responses are called for, which confounds the effect of any one of them and still does not give practice of the skill she needs.

Fastcheck 32

The response model

---

1 Decide whether the child should make either:

    A POINTING RESPONSE
  or A VERBAL RESPONSE
  or A 'TOUCH-AND-SAY' RESPONSE
  or A WRITTEN RESPONSE

2 Integrate this with the way in which you present the task, so that the child will need either to:

    SEE, THEN POINT
  or HEAR, THEN POINT
  or SEE, THEN SAY
  or HEAR, THEN SAY
  or SEE, THEN WRITE
  or HEAR, THEN WRITE
  or MAKE ANOTHER SUITABLE RESPONSE

> NOTE THAT THESE ARE ALL EASILY DETECTABLE RESPONSES

3 Immediately before you make the child respond to any new task, be prepared to demonstrate the correct response clearly, to emphasize the right way of going about the task and so reduce the probability of irrelevant responses.

FROM HERE GO TO STEP 3

Step 3   Probe the baseline level

STARTING POINT When learner, task, and the required response have been identified.

Outline The baseline is the level against which all future changes in performance will be judged, thus forming an essential component of performance evaluation, for without it there can be no measurable improvement and no specific predictions about later performance.

To assess the child's baseline status, administer a 'probe' or *mini-test* containing items relevant to the task selected, and which demands production of the response you have previously chosen. Items included in a given probe should be of comparable difficulty, i.e. the probe should be composed of a set of items of equal complexity. There should be more material than the child can get through in the time allowed, which for brevity will normally be *one minute*, although you could select a longer period if you thought it was important to do so. Do this for five days under the most consistent circumstances you can, for example using the same probe, in the same place, at the same time each day. Minimize the number of distractions present and try to eliminate any likely interruptions if possible.

COMPLETION POINT   When you have collected probe results for five consecutive days.

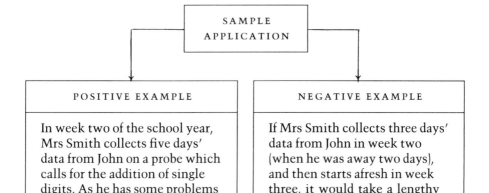

SAMPLE APPLICATION	
POSITIVE EXAMPLE	**NEGATIVE EXAMPLE**
In week two of the school year, Mrs Smith collects five days' data from John on a probe which calls for the addition of single digits. As he has some problems with this, she begins her teaching intervention in week three.	If Mrs Smith collects three days' data from John in week two (when he was away two days), and then starts afresh in week three, it would take a lengthy two weeks before some intervention started to help him to correct his errors.

Fastcheck 33	The baseline model

3.1 Have a probe sheet at hand containing more items than the learner can complete in the time available. A stopwatch, clock, or watch with sweep second hand will also be essential for timing purposes.

3.2 Take the child through a practice item. Remember that you then want to know what he can do *without* help, so after the practice item *do not model correct responses when probing performance.*

3.3 For *visual* (e.g. written) presentation, display the probe sheet, tell the child to start work, and begin timing simultaneously.

3.4 For *oral* presentation, say 'Get ready', then begin saying items and timing.

3.5 Note errors as they are produced. (*Make no comment or correction.*) This will generally be easier than trying to recall specific errors afterwards, especially when a lot of error responses are made.

3.6 Say 'Stop now' at the end of the time available for the probe and mark the point the child has reached. (*Avoid commenting on standard of work, say something neutral like* 'Fine', 'O.K.', *or* 'That's it'.)

3.7 Direct the child to the next activity in which you want him to engage.

FROM HERE GO TO STEP 4

Step 4 Measure performance

STARTING POINT When both the task and the learner's response have been identified.

Outline Right from the first day's work, score the child's responses to the chosen probe. The essential unit of measurement in Precision Teaching is that of *rate per minute*, the reason being that the rate of responding is a convenient index of the child's fluency. As Eaton (1978) pointed out, fluency often discriminates between recent acquisition of a skill and proficiency in its use, making increases in the rate of completion a time-scaled indication of learning progress.

In order to make full use of all the information we can derive from the child's performance, rates are computed for *correct* and *error* responses produced within the time allowed for the probe, and the results of both trends recorded day by day.

COMPLETION POINT When *correct* and *error* rates have been obtained for all five baseline days.

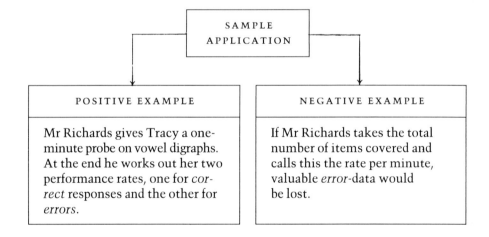

SAMPLE APPLICATION

POSITIVE EXAMPLE

Mr Richards gives Tracy a one-minute probe on vowel digraphs. At the end he works out her two performance rates, one for *correct* responses and the other for *errors*.

NEGATIVE EXAMPLE

If Mr Richards takes the total number of items covered and calls this the rate per minute, valuable *error*-data would be lost.

Fastcheck 34

The measurement model

4.1 As soon as the child has started to respond at your request, make a note of any *errors* made. This can be simply done by recording small vertical checkmarks in groups of four, crossing them through with a diagonal line for the fifth *error* (卌). An *error total* is derived by counting the groups of check-marks, e.g.:

卌 卌 = 10 errors

卌 卌 111 = 13 errors

卌 卌 卌 卌 卌 111 = 28 errors

4.2 Count how many responses were made altogether to get an *overall total*.

4.3 Subtract the *error total* from the *overall total*. The result is the *correct total*

> OVERALL TOTAL − ERROR TOTAL = CORRECT TOTAL

4.4 If you have administered a one-minute probe, those totals, derived from a single minute's performance, automatically give you *rate per minute*.

4.5 To obtain the same rate from a two-minute probe, divide *correct* and *error* totals each by two. A *correct* rate of eighty-two and an *error* rate of four on a two-minute probe would give rates per minute (RPM) of forty-one and two, respectively.

4.6 Keep your measurements simple as follows:

READING: Words per minute (WPM). Count any deviation from the text as an *error*.

WRITING: Letters per minute (LPM). Count any deviation from your model as an *error*.

MATHS: Digits per minute (DPM). Score each digit separately where answers have more than one digit.

If you refer now to FASTCHECK 35, you will see how this measurement model has been applied to certain basic skills where a child's *rate* of response can be taken to represent his level of proficiency.

Fastcheck 35

Scoring procedures from one-minute probes

READING RESPONSES

fast

girl *skates*

It was the first time that they had tried to grill steaks on

elephant *super*

the electric cooker at supper time. Both brother and

brother

sister went to a great deal of trouble after the butcher

flowing *recip*

had sent prime cuts of meat, following a recipe of their

mother's carefully. Indeed, because of their hunger, they

invented *present*

became so involved with the preparation of the meal

that they failed to notice how late it was, or that the

after

time for the arrival of the last bus was getting near.

LHT LHT I

ERROR WORDS

TOTAL	84
ERROR	11
CORRECT	73

WRITING RESPONSES

PROBE CONTENT COVERED:

Sid got up late on the morning of his birthday to find that the post had arrived. There were letters all over the floor by the letter box.

CHILD'S RESPONSE:

n *ir* *that*

Sid got up late on the mornig of his brithday to find the

r

post had arived. There

LHT III

ERROR LETTERS

TOTAL	63
ERROR	8
CORRECT	55

continued

MATHS RESPONSES

WRITE NUMBERS	1 2 3 4 5 6 ⑦ 8 ⑨ 10 11 12 13 14 15 16 1~~5~~ 18 1⑨ ⑩②	TOTAL 31 ERROR 5 CORRECT 26

LHI ERROR DIGITS

ADD SINGLE DIGITS		
3 2 4 5 3 6 5 6 7		TOTAL 11
+1 +2 +2 +3 +2 +3 +4 +6 +6		ERROR 1
4 4 6 8 5 9 9 12 ①②		CORRECT 10

① ERROR DIGITS

SUBTRACT WITH CARRY		
23 35 44 55 67 83		
−19 −16 −15 −36 −28 −39		TOTAL 11
⑧ ㉑ ㉛ ㉑ ㊶ ㊸		ERROR 10

LHI LHI ERROR DIGITS — CORRECT 1

FROM HERE GO TO STEP 5

Step 5   Chart baseline results

STARTING POINT   When *correct* and *error* rates are available for the first baseline day.

Outline Correct and *error* data from the baseline period are charted to provide a clear visual representation of developments throughout the period of measurement. On the type of chart used here, the horizontal axis represents time (each separate column is coded with a number representing one working day), while the vertical axis shows increases in the rate of performance from the bottom of the chart towards the top. (See the blank sample Progress Chart on page 108.)

The increments in rate are shown on a ratio scale which allows us to compare varying response rates in a way not possible on an ordinary arithmetic scale. (For example, a gain on oral reading rates from twenty to forty words per minute (WPM) correct shows the same acceleration factor as one from ten to twenty WPM, whereas on an arithmetic graph it would appear greater as an artifact of the scale.) At the bottom of the chart a trend table shows the rate data from *correct* and *error* performance each day, thus on the one sheet we have both numerical and visual representations of variation in the child's learning activity. (See Progress Chart, 'A' on page 110.)

COMPLETION POINT When five *correct* and five *error* plots have been entered on the child's progress chart.

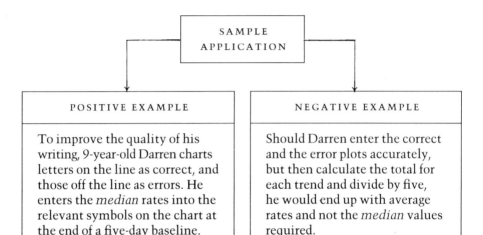

SAMPLE APPLICATION	
POSITIVE EXAMPLE	**NEGATIVE EXAMPLE**
To improve the quality of his writing, 9-year-old Darren charts letters on the line as correct, and those off the line as errors. He enters the *median* rates into the relevant symbols on the chart at the end of a five-day baseline.	Should Darren enter the correct and the error plots accurately, but then calculate the total for each trend and divide by five, he would end up with average rates and not the *median* values required.

PROGRESS CHART
(SAMPLE)

name:	task:
supervisor:	response:
date started:	date completed:

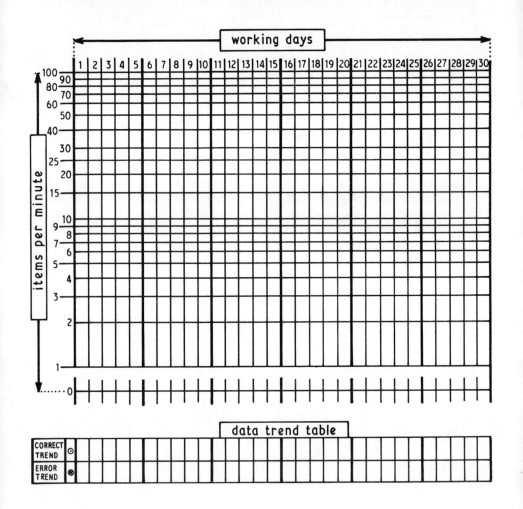

working days

1 2 3 4 5 6 7 8 9 10 11 12 13 14 15 16 17 18 19 20 21 22 23 24 25 26 27 28 29 30

items per minute

100 90 80 70 60 50 40 30 25 20 15 10 9 8 7 6 5 4 3 2 1 0

data trend table

CORRECT TREND	⊙																													
ERROR TREND	⊗																													

Fastcheck 36

The baseline charting model

5.1 Enter performance data into the trend table and chart each day.

5.2 Enter CORRECT TREND data plots on chart as dots. Surround each dot with a small circle (☉). Connect dots with a solid line (☉—☉—☉—☉).

5.3 Enter ERROR TREND data plots on chart as crosses. Surround each cross with a small circle (⊗). Connect crosses with solid lines (⊗—⊗—⊗).

5.4 Check that the data plots tally with the performance figures for both trends in the trend table.

5.5 Enter a vertical line (a *phase line*) at the left-hand edge of the graph which runs to a point just above the highest rate achieved, then continue horizontally until it spans the final day of baseline performance. Write 'BASELINE' in printed letters over the top. All phase lines denote the phase of learner activity with which you are dealing.

5.6 Find the middle rates (*medians*) for the *correct* and *error trends* by writing their respective data in *ascending order* and putting a circle around the central item. The middle in a series of five different values is always the third one, hence the median rate will occur in this position. It is used as a measure of the central tendency in the child's performance, i.e. a representative value, and is less affected by extreme values than an average would be.

5.7 In a convenient position beneath the CORRECT TREND data plots on the chart show the central tendency as a symbol drawn like this (♀) and write the median value inside it, e.g. 40.

5.8 Repeat this procedure for the ERROR TREND data plots, *inverting* the symbol (♂).

PROGRESS CHART
(CHART 'A')

name: MICHAEL	task: CURSIVE HANDWRITING
supervisor: HEATHER	response: WRITE CORRECTLY JOINED LETTERS ON LINE
date started: 12-9-85	date completed: 12-10-85

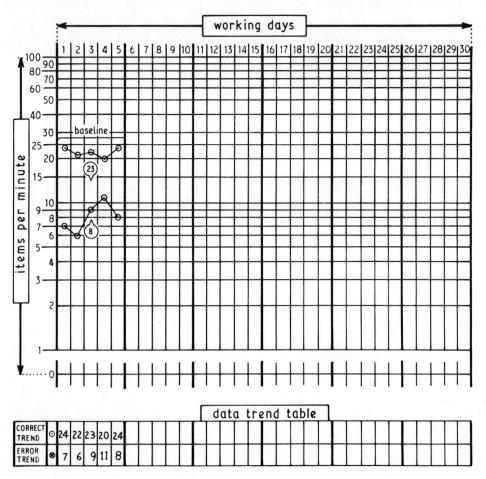

working days

items per minute

data trend table

CORRECT TREND ⊙	24	22	23	20	24																									
ERROR TREND ⊛	7	6	9	11	8																									

FROM HERE GO TO STEP 6

Step 6 Predict future performance

STARTING POINT   When *median* rates have been computed for both correct and error baseline trends.

Outline Prediction needs to relate the current standard of performance to some future level which provides an aim for the child to work towards, hence we normally plan that the *correct* rate should go higher and the *error* rate become lower. If the correct rate went up *and* the error rate followed, accuracy would become reduced by increased speed of response. If the error rate drops and the correct rate also falls, then it may be inferred that the learner is being unduly cautious, or does not understand what to do. Clearly, neither of these outcomes is as desirable as an increase in correct rate matched by a decrease in error rate – hence it is upon this outcome that predictions are based.

The essential issue is how much change to predict in how much time. If we set too high a *target rate* in too short a time, then it will prove impossible for the learner to achieve, and the result would very likely be frustration all round. Should we set the target rate too low and allow too much time, then we run the risk of boredom setting in. To increase the likelihood of successful prediction, an appropriate criterion can be selected from the set which follows:

CRITERION A: MINIMAL CHANGE

The proposed rate of growth for *minimal change* is that of an overall 5 per cent for each day between start and finish of the learning period, an easy figure to calculate, and one which approximates to the minimal change factor of 1.25 highlighted by Liberty (1975) from a review of 361 precision programmes.

At an overall 5 per cent the prediction would involve a 25 per cent improvement in performance over a one-week period, 50 per cent if the instructional period were two weeks, and 100 per cent during a four-week programme if minimal change were to be maintained. More rapid rates may ultimately prove to be within the child's grasp, but this is a relatively straightforward method for introducing planned growth and therefore the one recommended for initial exploration. Should the child easily exceed this rate of improvement, transfer to a more suitable rate may be effected by selecting one of the other criteria mentioned.

CRITERION B: TIME AVAILABLE

This is a most economical technique, for one takes the number of work days available until the next school holiday and then uses the last working day as the target date, fitting the work to be done into the resulting time-scale. One possible drawback is that, early in the school term, this may allow too much time and thus only require sub-standard performance which the child could easily better. This criterion is therefore not recommended where it allows the child to drop below the 'minimal' change threshold. Another problem can arise late on in the school term, when too few working days remain to allow the child to achieve mastery of the learning sequence, and consequently *time available* should also be avoided when it would take an adult level of competency to complete the task in the number of working days left.

CRITERION C: ADULT COMPARISON

Adults generally out-perform children on basic learning tasks, and clearly it is desirable for a child to move towards adult levels of competency, hence an alternative strategy is to find out how soon an adult might achieve the target rates, and then allow some extra time for the child to reach the same standard. Two problems exist in trying to do this and one of these lies in the greater experience of the adult, while the other lies in trying to ascertain what extra proportion of the time taken should be allowed for the child. Since we do not at present understand how consistent the relationship between adult and child performance may be, or how stable it is over different tasks, one could have reservations about how valid this criterion may be, and it is suggested that its use be kept on an experimental basis.

CRITERION D: PEER COMPARISON

This could perhaps be seen as a slightly fairer criterion than adult comparison as it ought to be easier to find another child like the one we are trying to help. Ideally, of course, we want a typical peer, but individual differences in children's performance may narrow down the choice to a point where we are no longer dealing with comparable children, so that an ideal match may prove difficult to find. For *peer comparison* the target peer would clearly need to be the child who could offer the most similar performance characteristics on the task to be mastered. However, because of the arbitrary nature of the peer-selection process, it would perhaps be safest to view this criterion as simply offering a rule-of-thumb.

A safer level of peer comparison may be found in a situation where data is available from the performance of several peers on the task in hand. Although there will inevitably be variation in the individual rates obtained, this can to some extent be balanced out by calculating a measure of central tendency, such as the *median* rate, and taking this as the index of prediction for the child with whom you are working. The chief assumption here is, of course, that such data have already been gathered and this is probably unlikely in many situations, because of the very diversity of learning tasks and the wide range of individual learning difficulties encountered in practice. However, it may be worthwhile in the longer term attempting to develop such a data-bank on routine tasks, should you feel adventurous!

CRITERION E: SELF-COMPARISON

Of all levels of comparison, this could well be the fairest, in so far as the yardstick for prediction is derived from the same individual, and this could be particularly important for any child who is sensitive about unfavourable comparison with anyone else. The important thing, as with other methods of comparison, is to obtain the best match possible, so that we can relate like to like. In this instance it will mean predicting target levels on a new task from those obtained on a completed task which has the most similar attributes one can find. If we base the prediction on an unrelated task which called for a dissimilar response, it will necessarily entail more risk and be of questionable validity.

If you refer to Progress Chart 'B' on page 116, you will see that the prediction model has been followed according to the minimal-change criterion referred to in the text, and this criterion will probably be the easiest one for you to apply as well, at least until a reasonable amount of rate measurement data has been accumulated on children with whom you are working.

Summary of criteria:
A Minimal change
B Time available
C Adult comparison
D Peer comparison
E Self-comparison

COMPLETION POINT   When two aim stars have been entered on the Progress Chart, and a guideline drawn in connecting each one with its start mark.

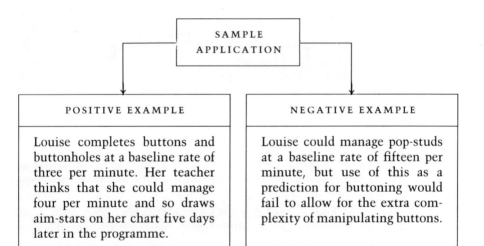

SAMPLE APPLICATION

POSITIVE EXAMPLE

Louise completes buttons and buttonholes at a baseline rate of three per minute. Her teacher thinks that she could manage four per minute and so draws aim-stars on her chart five days later in the programme.

NEGATIVE EXAMPLE

Louise could manage pop-studs at a baseline rate of fifteen per minute, but use of this as a prediction for buttoning would fail to allow for the extra complexity of manipulating buttons.

Fastcheck 37	**The prediction model**

6.1 Within the five-day *baseline* phase, pinpoint where the *middle day* and *middle rate* intersect on the *correct trend*. Enter a *starting point* (⊕) where the lines cross.

This will always be at the junction of the third day and the *median rate*.

6.2 Repeat 6.1 for the *starting point* on the *error trend*.

6.3 Using the 5 per cent rule for *minimal change*, locate the day on which the *target rate* will be reached and enter an *aim star* ✸ here for the *correct trend*. The centre of the *aim star* marks the intersection of *target rate* and *target date*.

6.4 Repeat 6.3 to enter an *aim star* ✸ for the *error trend*.

6.5 Connect *starting point* to *aim star* with a dotted line on the *correct trend*. Because it links up varying rates of performance, this line represents the *guideline* towards future mastery of the task.

6.6 Connect *starting point* to *aim star* with a dotted line for the *guide-line* on the *error trend*.

6.7 Note that, since an increase (for *correct trend*) and a decrease (for *error trend*) in performance are involved on the same task, the *guidelines* will diverge.

PROGRESS CHART
(CHART 'B')

name: MICHAEL	task: CURSIVE HANDWRITING
supervisor: HEATHER	response: WRITE CORRECTLY JOINED LETTERS ON LINE
date started: 12-9-85	date completed: 12-10-85

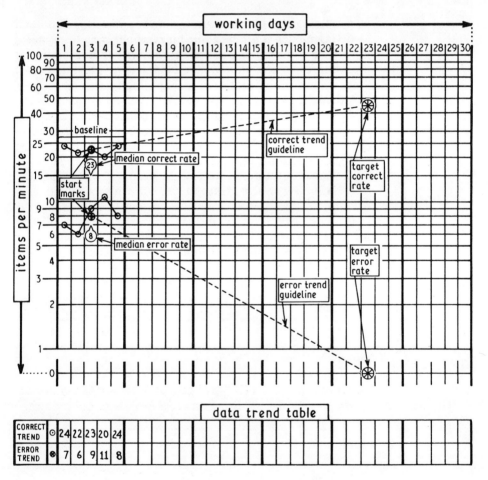

FROM HERE GO TO STEP 7

Step 7 Commence intervention

STARTING POINT When target levels and procedures for instruction have been decided upon.

Outline In this phase of the learning programme we are no longer so concerned with what the child has *already* learned (as we were during the *baseline* phase), but we do want to know how far he can *change* his learning performance. For this purpose the aim is to employ only one method of presentation at a time, so that we find out whether it promotes optimal growth in performance. Where we decide that a particular procedure does not work well enough, a new phase is started using a relevant alternative.

Although daily probing continues throughout the programme, an important feature of *intervention* is to move from probing only (as during baseline) to a *'probe-and-learn'* strategy. From the baseline results we have a measure of the child's existing performance, and from the *prediction* we have a *target* for improvement, so we are at this stage concerned with organizing our resources to bridge the gap as efficiently as possible.

From the point of view of initial instruction, each day the individual should spend a short but highly focused period learning how to correct his existing error responses with the aid of a *supervisor* who has already mastered the skill concerned and can consistently model correct responses. (This person need not necessarily be the teacher, provided that he or she can follow verbal or written instructions relevant to the sequence being learned.) Such an approach will help the learner to become accurate and, once that has been achieved, fluency can then be built up by practising the relevant responses more rapidly.

COMPLETION POINT When the child has reached or exceeded the *target rates* for three consecutive days.

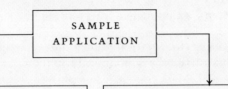

POSITIVE EXAMPLE	NEGATIVE EXAMPLE
Mrs Furbank notes that Wayne's correct rate for calculating percentages is in excess of her prediction by day nine, but his error rate is also more than predicted for days seven, eight and nine. She therefore institutes a new phase of instruction, maintaining it until the error rate stays at the level aimed at for over three days.	If Mrs Furbank just lets Wayne go on to find his own level, there is a danger that he will learn to sacrifice accuracy for speed, which will not make him more proficient.

Fastcheck 38	**The intervention model**

7.1 Keep probing performance and charting results each day.

7.2 Once the daily probe has been completed, provide the child with a daily learning assignment based on the errors produced and calling for the same mode of response as the probe sheet. Monitor this, either yourself or through a competent helper who will work as *supervisor* under your directions.

7.3 During the assignment, the supervisor should avoid criticizing the child's errors, but immediately following each one should say what is incorrect and *model* the *correct response*.

7.4 After modelling, the supervisor directs the *learner* to repeat the correct response at the same time, i.e. *do it together*.

7.5 Once a supervisor and learner have done it together, direct the learner to do it *alone*.

7.6 Do this until the learner can make three consecutive *correct responses*.

7.7 Mark this period of activity on the chart with a *phase line* set in vertically at the beginning of the Intervention period, and running across the top for the full duration. Remember to label it concisely over the top, so that at a later date you can refer back to what you did and quickly determine what happened. This can form a useful reference when you come to work with other children with the same kind of problem.

FROM HERE GO TO STEP 8

Step 8 Evaluate the outcomes

STARTING POINT   On day three of the *intervention* phase of your programme.

Outline   As the intervention unfolds, the resulting data plots will extend further across the child's chart, and the pattern the connecting line makes along the data plots for each of the two trends represented will be a function of how rapidly he learns. This line is therefore known as the *line of progress*.

While the line of progress stays *on or above* the *correct-trend guideline*, also *on or below* the *error-trend guideline*, no change is needed in the method of instruction. Keep it going until the learner has stabilized at the target rates.

Where the line of progress drops *below* the correct-trend guideline, or climbs *above* the error-trend guideline, evidence of failure is beginning to accrue. Failure should be eliminated quickly by modifying one aspect of the learning situation at a time, in which case we start a *new phase* of learner activity for each modification introduced, labelling the chart accordingly.

By referring to Progress Chart 'C' you can see that the complete data has been plotted from a modestly successful precision programme of twenty-two days' duration (five days baseline plus seventeen days' instruction) for learning to write cursive script. Locate for yourself the following features:

1 The BASELINE data plots.
2 The baseline MEDIANS.
3 The STARTING POINTS on both trends.
4 The TARGET RATES on both trends.
5 The respective GUIDELINES.
6 The respective LINES OF PROGRESS.
7 The labelled PHASE LINES.
8 The final MEDIANS.

As you can observe, the *correct trend* and *error trend* data plots begin fairly close together, but end up relatively far apart – the classic divergent shift derived from true learning progress. Note also the annotations relating to specific attributes of the chart, and in particular that a new learning phase was immediately introduced when the *error rate* crept above the planned level in the first week of instruction. This chart demonstrates an effective use of teacher correction in helping a child, in this case Michael, reduce his error rate while maintaining the acceleration of *correct* responses.

While in the course of your work you will inevitably tackle more complex skills, Progress Chart 'C', in showing progress on a low-level task, offers a clear picture of how learning can be mapped out in the form of a coherent and objective record. In doing this, it demonstrates how the Progress Chart can offer powerful evidence of change taking place through the medium of direct daily measurement, a principle which applies equally well to more sophisticated skills.

COMPLETION POINT   When all the data have been plotted on the *Progress Chart* and outline notes written on each phase.

POSITIVE EXAMPLE	NEGATIVE EXAMPLE
Lorna's oral reading performance reaches a plateau just below the target rate set by her teacher, Mr Tompkins. Then he starts to model each paragraph for her, and rewards daily improvement by giving her points towards a favourite activity. This attention to instruction and motivation produces the desired effect and she exceeds the targets set for three days.	If Mr Tompkins had made no adjustment to the conditions for learning in Lorna's case, this would probably have had an adverse effect on her motivation for the task in hand.

PROGRESS CHART

(CHART 'c')

name: MICHAEL	task: CURSIVE HANDWRITING
supervisor: HEATHER	response: WRITE CORRECTLY JOINED LETTERS ON LINE
date started: 12-9-85	date completed: 12-10-85

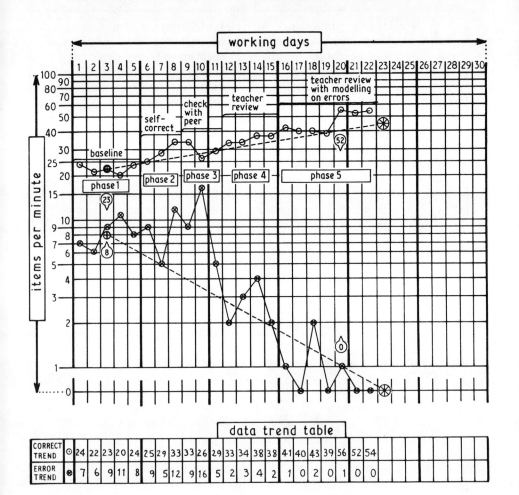

CORRECT TREND	⊙	24	22	23	20	24	25	29	33	33	26	29	33	34	38	38	41	40	43	39	56	52	54							
ERROR TREND	✳	7	6	9	11	8	9	5	12	9	16	5	2	3	4	2	1	0	2	0	1	0	0							

The evaluation model

8.1 Check that *lines of progress* match or exceed your *guideline* predictions for both *correct* and *error* performance rates, from day three of your *intervention* onwards.

8.2 Where this continues up to the *target rates,* have the learner *hold* for *three consecutive days.* This hold period will represent a more reliable indication of stable performance than just a one-day check.

8.3 Should evidence of *failure* emerge on three consecutive days for *either or both trends,* start a *new phase* of learner activity.

8.4 Review your task selection, instruction, and *aim date,* then decide whether it is a component of the learning programme which needs changing, or something about the child's existing level of motivation.

8.5 Changes in learning may involve shifting to an easier task, revising the mode of presentation and/or the mode of response, giving different directions, demonstrating more often, demanding more practice, or providing stronger cues, e.g. speaking more clearly or writing more boldly. Refer back to earlier sections of the text here as the need arises.

8.6 Changing a child's motivation may mean increasing the amount of eye contact or physical contact when the individual approximates to the response you want; giving more frequent social rewards like smiles or verbal praise when he makes some effort; or employing tangible rewards like stars, points, or consumable goodies in response to greater effort. While younger children often respond best to tangible rewards, there is no hard and fast formula for this, so be prepared to experiment until you find what works best in your classroom, which is, after all, unique in certain respects. The golden rule is that effort should come *before* reward, in order to avoid bribery!

SUMMARY OF STEPS TAKEN

Step 1: Pinpoint the task
Step 2: Select the learner's response
Step 3: Establish a baseline
Step 4: Measure performance
Step 5: Chart baseline results
Step 6: Predict future performance
Step 7: Commence intervention
Step 8: Evaluate the outcome

From the eight steps outlined, it can be seen that a direct, objective and individualized technique for measuring learning progress has become available, which opens up some exciting possibilities for teachers of children with persistent learning difficulties, not the least of which is a chance to realize the elusive ideal of continuous assessment. Progress Charts incorporating rate measurements can be used to analyse educational performance on a developmental basis. By portraying the unfolding trends in a child's learning, they can help towards more efficient time-management in the classroom. They can be used for rapid diagnosis of learning problems with the need to refer to external support services initially. They can store a great deal of information regarding the efficacy of reinforcement procedures, which is also of significance for the design and evaluation of future learning programmes and is potentially useful for the placement of children within those programmes. Last, but not least, they can provide substantial background material for liaison with a given child's parents, and be helpful in working out projects which involve an aide working with children under teacher supervision.

A degree of caution none the less seems appropriate, since any attempt at the blanket application of rate measurements in all curriculum areas and across all children could be unwieldy and unduly time-consuming. Spelling and comprehension tasks are probably unsuitable as the need for accuracy predominates in each case. *Daily* measurement may be regarded as an ideal rather than an absolute necessity, the closest approximation which can be achieved in practice providing the optimum reality. The demand for thoroughness of organization increases in proportion to the number of probe sheets, progress charts, and sets of teaching materials which have to be maintained. There are as yet no consistently agreed estimates of how well children should be able to perform even basic skills in terms of their rate of responding. For these and other more technical reasons it would seem advisable to restrict the use of precision teaching to either a particular programme or a limited number of children if you are exploring its potential for the first time.

Review eight

DIRECTIONS

To check the extent of your understanding at this point, it is recommended that you attempt to answer all ten questions in the review *before* you look up any of the answers supplied. All of the questions are derived from the text, but you may find some a little harder than others.

REVIEW QUESTIONS

1 What is the main difference between a rate and an accuracy measurement?
2 Identify two features to look for in selecting a given learning task.
3 Name one advantage of selecting a specific response for the learner to produce.
4 Should you model correct responses when measuring a child's baseline performance?
5 For which variables should you calculate rate measurements: the total number of responses, correct responses only, correct and error responses, or error responses only?
6 On a three-minute probe in which he has to name letters presented at random, Tim responds correctly 156 times and makes nine errors. What are his correct and error rates on this task?
7 How do you calculate the median rate for five different days' performance data?

8 Name four of the criteria by which a child's future performance may be predicted.
9 During an intervention phase, would you initially seek to build up accuracy or fluency?
10 When you look at a Progress Chart, how can you determine whether or not a child has mastered the task to be learned?

GUIDELINES

After attempting all ten questions, compare your responses with the answers given for this purpose. An acceptable mastery level for Review Eight is nine answers correct. It is suggested that you look through the text related to any incorrect responses. (Page numbers are listed against the answers in the Answers to Reviews section, pages 141–6, to help you do this quickly.) If you have less than eight answers correct, it is likely that you will profit from re-reading the preceding section for a fuller understanding.

9

Preparing the programme environment

1 If you are going to design a programme of your own

1.1 Stop! It is not recommended that you begin with a single-handed venture. An exercise of this kind would be far better undertaken as a cooperative project. The first step should be to find someone else (not necessarily from your own school) who shares your intended goal and who would be prepared to work with you on a project which, to be fair, should be of mutual benefit. If you can, assemble a small project team which would be willing to meet at least weekly, composed of teachers or people from external support services. Cooperating with other people will make the workload more manageable and less time-consuming.

1.2 Take charge yourself – this makes it more likely that you will end up with what *you* want, rather than what *someone else* thinks you ought to have – it's your project after all. Notwithstanding this, be prepared to delegate responsibility for discrete objectives to others. When you meet to work on the programme, do just that – avoid wasting time in lengthy social chit-chat, which can stretch meeting time beyond comfortable limits. There will always be time for social interchange beyond this.

1.3 Try to start with something *simple*: there are no medals to be won for incurring ulcers on your first attempt! Remember the slogan: 'Simple is efficient.' What you learn can always be applied to larger projects later on, whereas, if you start with something on a grand scale, it is likely that the demands of coordinating the various components will put you off for life! It will also help you to manage things if you work to some acceptable timescale, i.e. agree the timing and duration of your meetings, and set a target date for completion of the programme.

1.4 When you agree the programme goal, list the competencies children will need to achieve it. At this stage, it will be helpful if you consult as many of the following sources as you can, relative to your particular goal:

(a) Previously used learning materials
(b) Published schemes of work in the same area
(c) Suggestions from other teachers
(d) Curriculum information from other schools
(e) Entry requirements for the next relevant class
(f) Current performance data from the children.

Again, it will prove less onerous if you can find a way to share some of these tasks and focus the attention of everyone involved upon the need to extract material selectively, so that you end up with only the amount and quality of information which is relevant for your own purpose.

1.5 Apply the design guidelines described earlier in the text, and any others with which you may be familiar, to shape the programme content. If possible, it is a good idea to have two people work on each portion for mutual support in any case, e.g. one to write it and one to read it, or one to write a first draft and the other to write a second draft. It will probably be desirable to assign final responsibility for each major feature (e.g. the directions, the illustrations, choice of examples, the opening lesson, the lesson sequence, etc.) to one colleague, so that each individual's responsibilities are defined.

1.6 Decide how and when you will measure the competencies the programme sets out to establish. Select from:

(a) Measures of *accuracy*
(Percentage accuracy is useful for many situations and already widely used.)

(b) Measures of *rate*
(Rate measurements are useful for oral reading, arithmetic, writing and physical skills, to give a developmental index of proficiency.

You will be well advised to plan for repeated measures, so that trends in learning performance can be highlighted across time, so decide how often to measure, and how measures should be applied, e.g. by:

I Class teacher
II Another teacher
III A teacher's aide
IV A parent volunteer
V Another child
VI Self-recording by the learner

Having made these decisions, design an individual and/or group record sheet upon which the results will be tabulated, so that you can refer back to a given child's performance when, say, writing a report or seeking information for someone else who has a direct interest in how the child is getting on.

1.7 A related issue, the *entry test*, arises where your programme covers a range of skills with varying levels of difficulty. Children inevitably differ in their existing competencies and it is desirable to allow for these in relation to the programme. One way of achieving an optimal match between child and programme is to select some items from each of the various levels in order to screen the child before you start to teach him or her, so that he or she is more likely to enter the programme at the right level.

Naturally, any child who passes all the items in the entry test will probably need somewhat more advanced work, whereas one who fails some or all of them will be likely to need the programme started at some other point. Total failure may indicate that a lower level of programme content is needed, or at least that certain foundation skills need to be taught first.

1.8 Before attempting widespread implementation of your programme, try it out selectively. This can best be achieved through a phased induction procedure such as the one shown below:

PHASE I: Review the programme alone.

PHASE II: Try a sample of the programme on a colleague who helped you with the design and who understands what your aim is.

PHASE III: Try a representative portion of the programme on a colleague who was not involved in the design process.

PHASE IV: Teach a sample of the programme to just one child with whom you are familiar, and who you think will be able to respond appropriately.

PHASE V: Teach the whole programme to a small group of children who need to learn the skills involved.

It is, of course, important to make sure that you are familiar with the content for any given task before you attempt to teach it. Moreover, it will be crucial for developing the effectiveness of your programme that you build in modifications which are highlighted through all phases of the *induction* period.

1.9 Establish a plan of action for any child who will not be included in the programme, so that interruptions will be minimized. Such a plan should include:

(a) An alternative assignment
(b) Materials such as pencils, paper, work-cards, reference books, tape recorder, or computer
(c) Clear directions about how to do the assignment
(d) Definite instructions about what to do upon completion
(e) A back-up task to employ any waiting time productively
(f) Planned rewards for productive work.

2 If you are going to evaluate a new programme

2.1 The ideal situation is one where you can 'try before you buy'. However, this is sometimes difficult to achieve and you may be limited to leafing through a catalogue, or, a little more usefully, have an opportunity to look through a copy of the programme. One alternative is, of course, to look for an independent source of information, and a relatively easy way of doing this is probably to talk to someone in your district who may use the programme in which you are interested. (Although opinions of several users will probably give a more balanced picture.)

The chief advantage of this latter course of action is that you can not only find out about details of the programme, but also collect valuable impressions from people who have first-hand experience of using it. Personnel from teacher-support services should be able to help you find out whether a given programme is in use in your locality.

Nevertheless, in the final analysis, there must come a point at which you have to decide upon whether the programme will justify your intended investment of both money and professional time. This in turn poses the question of how you might separate the wheat from the chaff, and it is suggested that there are three levels at which much of this screening can be carried out.

Level I   Major design strategies
A Does the programme as it stands facilitate evaluation by either: (a) Published field-test data to indicate whether children learned the skills to be taught? *or* (b) Including direct skill measures which will allow you to develop your own data base? B Is the programme based upon direct teaching and assessment in the classroom? C Is it centred upon teacher-led activities in which foundation skills are given initial priority?

D Is there specific guidance on the presentation of the material for each separate task involved?

E Is skills-induction begun with multiple cues for the learner which are gradually faded out entirely?

F Is there a model for each verbal and non-verbal skill involved?

G Does extensive practice feature as part of the skills-induction process?

H Are skills maintained and reviewed beyond the induction phase?

I Are there examples showing what corrections to undertake when children go wrong for each type of task covered?

J Do the sequences follow the principle of teaching *identification* responses before *production* responses?

Level II   Tactical procedures

A Are the presentation routines held constant across equivalent tasks?

B Is a range of positive and negative examples supplied for each important rule?

C Is the learner required to apply each rule in a practice sequence?

D Do the examples given actually illustrate the essential rules?

E Does the programme provide demonstration *and* practice routines in parallel with each other?

F Is the terminology unambiguous?

G Do the directions clearly describe the task in hand?

H Do the directions make it clear to the learner how he should respond?

I Do suggested questions fall within the range of the content taught?

J Does the programme emphasize teacher-recognition of learner application to the task?

The range of criteria at Levels I and II is by no means exhaustive; however, if you can find a programme with most of these features, it is more likely to be good value for money. The likelihood is that designers of the programme have paid careful attention to detail and have systematically applied important design principles which will promote learning progress.

Level III   Contra-indications

A   In general, absence of Level I and Level II features would cast doubt on the efficacy of the programme.
B   Any loosely portrayed examples which would permit of a variety of possible interpretations or responses.
C   Examples which violate the rules taught.
D   Lack of association between information (written or verbal) and any pictorial representation used.
E   Introduction of new tasks before practice and mastery of preparatory items.
F   The inclusion of irrelevant material or discussion.
G   Absence of procedures which provide for recognition of learner effort.
H   Failure to provide a record-keeping facility.
I   The absence of an entry test for placing the child in the programme.
J   The omission of specific directions for follow-up of the programme.

If a programme exhibits many Level III features it is not likely to offer a worthwhile return on either your capital investment or your teaching time. Treat it with considerable caution, and also review the competition, as more than one publisher may produce comparable material. You might also reconsider whether you couldn't do a better job by exploiting local resources – only buy if you can modify!

The term 'programme' has crept into increasingly common use in educational circles, and for the lay person may carry an aura of intricacy and special knowledge. For the committed teacher, however, effectiveness cannot be determined through

Fastcheck 40	How do you manage programme issues?
	1 Do you review the programme materials before teaching begins? 2 Do you elicit the views of other users? 3 Can you derive a clear picture of the design strategies? 4 Can you determine what tactical teaching procedures are employed? 5 Are you able to list any contra-indications? 6 Do you know who will be working with you? 7 Is it clear just when you will work together and what each adult will do? 8 Is it apparent what the children should be able to do at the end? 9 Have you agreed how children will be allowed to enter into and exit from the programme? 10 Have you planned some consistent classroom-management procedures?

mystique, and a more appropriate professional viewpoint must be that a programme is as good as the learning that it engenders in the child. Learning is an interactive process, and the degree to which it results from a given programme largely derives from the extent to which appropriate design techniques have been applied. Skilful design is a major precursor of productive learning outcomes. For children who have difficulties in learning, careful design can clarify the information which they have to process and the response they are expected to produce, thereby reducing the cognitive demands of the learning task involved. However, achieving exemplary levels of design in specialized educational programmes is not an easy undertaking in our present state of knowledge, thus a practical balance must be sought between the amount of time available and curriculum and child variables. Since it is not within the scope of this book to present an exhaustive theoretical analysis of the associated problems, the purpose of the outline discussed in this chapter should be understood as that of providing a set of operational guidelines, to enable more conspicuous design issues to be addressed from a teacher's perspective and stimulate closer scrutiny of the content of existing programmes from the point of view of an unsophisticated learner.

Conclusion

Recent moves towards the development of less categorized provision for children with special needs is testimony to a belief that significant numbers of children may require particularly skilled help at some time during their school career. (If the Warnock upper estimate of one child in five is valid, then in a UK school population of around 9 million, as many as 1.8 million children could be involved.) The weight of argument here is that particular emphasis should be given to *what* form that help takes; *where* the help is given is regarded as being of less importance. It is also proposed that the capacity to provide appropriate learning programmes (in accordance with the expectations stated in official policy) should be highlighted as the central component of a teacher's expertise. Every child with special needs now has the right of access to effective educational programmes, and parents are paying for this privilege through their contributions to the cost of local-government services, amongst which education is by far the most costly.

When a child fails to learn in school, this signifies a kind of interaction between the child and the curriculum which may say as much about the programme of learning tasks involved as it does about the characteristics of the learner. Sometimes radical changes will be needed. Since any one of a complex of programme variables could be implicated when failure occurs, it seems logical to regard teacher intervention as essential for resolving persistent learning difficulties. While we can recognize that children may learn to some extent from each other, or sometimes even alone, a recurrence of problems is evidence of the need for a more astute level of assistance. Since teachers are older, have more real-world experience, possess a greater store of knowledge and have received an input of training, schools are basically where children learn and teachers teach. A good teacher will accelerate learning progress much more systematically than an individual child who has limited understanding and/or markedly variable motivation or behaviour. From a strictly pedagogical viewpoint, it can be argued that the chief justification for servicing special needs is that children progress as a result of the instruction they receive, and presumably this is a basic tenet in the philosophy of all teachers working in the special-needs sector.

In so far as the calibre of the interaction between child and curriculum is largely determined by the way in which any given learning programme is set up and presented, the development of design skills would represent a significant step in professional growth for teachers, as Branwhite and Levey (1982) previously suggested. One might venture to suggest that this could even represent a revised paradigm for special-needs provision, which could lead to a more rounded view of children's learning than can be derived from a single emphasis on either individual differences, behavioural objectives, task analysis, or curriculum development *per se*. Already a *legal* paradigm shift, affecting the way in which special educational services are being administered, has been imposed upon teachers, so perhaps the time is ripe to entertain a professional paradigm shift in which the *instructional* expertise of teachers is recognized as being of paramount importance. In educational terms there is little to be gained from preparing specialist staff to be child-minders, therapists, and social-workers as well as teachers.

Given that the overall aim is to resolve learning problems that have not proved amenable to conventional approaches, answers are more likely to be found through carefully designed instructional strategies than by any other means. (Educational technology should not be assumed to hold the key.) It is not that this would automatically be a panacea, for much remains to be learned about just how programme and learner variables can be made to interact in the most productive manner. However, within any domain where the onus is likely to be upon skills development, due regard for fundamental design principles (of which a far from exhaustive list has been presented here) seems likely to assist teachers in helping children to learn more effectively.

The special-needs sector benefits considerably from the commitment of teachers who possess a strong sense of vocation in fulfilling what is now one of the most demanding roles in teaching. One current problem for some of these teachers can be that they are aware of a lack of relevant skills because their training has not given enough attention to the development of instructional techniques. This problem was the focus of a discussion by Desforges and McNamara (1979) who commented that the practical aspects of teaching had long been the Cinderella of teacher education in the eyes of academics, and consequently they suggested that a need exists for real issues to be examined during training, rather than what they saw as 'the straw men' set up by much contemporary educational theory.

Roehler and Duffy (1981) took this point further, by citing what they called triple failures in teacher education. The first of these they identified as the relative lack of attention which was given to the complexity of classroom life. (Teachers have to contend with the occurrence of a large number of interacting classroom variables, not all of which are predictable in onset, intensity or duration.) The second, they said, was that proportionately little effort had been applied to training teachers in techniques for assisting children in their attempts to learn. (During a typical day, however, there will be many instances when learning events which children do not initially understand have to be made more comprehensible by a teacher.) Thirdly, preparation for applying instructional materials in ways which would support learning activity on the part of the child was also described as lacking effectiveness. (In using commercial materials, teachers may be relying upon programmes which are adequate until a child fails to learn, at which point a lack of advice can become apparent.) Teaching is far more than assigning children to learning materials and expecting that they will achieve mastery for themselves – it requires direct professional intervention rather than plain provision of learning opportunities. If these criticisms are valid, it would seem to be incumbent upon those involved with the pre-service or in-service training of teachers to update their knowledge, so that recent advances in the design and implementation of learning programmes can be spread more rapidly. In this area, background knowledge and application skills are arguably of equal importance, implying that a sharp distinction between theoretician and practitioner may be counter-productive.

It is one thing for the system of knowledge within teacher education to broadcast theoretical concepts freely, but quite another to arrive at a point where these concepts are transmitted in a form which is capable of being received *and* understood *and* have functional value. Most educators would recognize that a one-way flow of information is in itself unlikely to achieve this purpose, if for no other reason than that its relationship with real-world classroom issues may be weak. An interactive system of communication is professionally more appropriate (i.e. an interchange based upon shared concerns and a shared language) and is more capable of producing identifiable benefits for children, the primary consumers of educational services. A focus upon design considerations could contribute towards the development of such a system. The value of this step would lie in the fact that the special-needs sector is likely to be best served by individuals who are able to translate theory comprehensively into practice, and who in this time of financial constraint can also select the most cost-effective programmes for classroom use. An additional benefit to be derived from heightened sensitivity to the total context of instruction is that it could help to expand the frontiers of educational theory, by providing realistic feedback about the nature of the interaction between child and curriculum.

No doubt such propositions will appear controversial, like many others relating to improved provision for meeting special needs, but there is nothing new about controversy in educational circles. During the development of the State-education system, teachers have always had to do their work against an evolving knowledge base, which has sometimes produced very different styles of operation in the classroom. It has aptly been said, for instance, that:

> Today ... anyone who ventures to open his mouth ... to discuss principles and methods may well speak in fear and trembling. The most opposite opinions are maintained on every branch of school practice, and these opinions are concerned not only with trivial matters of school management, but they reach down to the fundamental doctrines of mind and morals, which consciously or unconsciously mould the thought of every teacher. Now, while this situation should warn us against the assumption of dogmatism, it cannot surely justify us in closing the door to study and research. If controversy abounds, all the more reason for encouraging teachers to investigate the principles of their art for themselves. . . .

While this advice has an important message for any contemporary teacher who wishes to resolve learning difficulties, it is salutary to realize that these words were, in fact, written during the last century, in a Special Report of the Board of Education in London, published by Her Majesty's Stationery Office in 1898. In some respects it may seem that little has changed. Today, however, we have the advantage of conducting our investigations in an era when the principles of productive teaching are being described in a more explicit manner than ever before, and wider recognition is being given to the need for programmes which are truly 'special'.

Answers to reviews

2.3 Any three of these items: visual perception, auditory perception, perceptual-motor ability, psycholinguistic ability.   20

2.4 Covert. They cannot be seen happening any more than can information-processing inside a computer.   19

2.5 They must be inferred from the child's behaviour.   22

2.6 No. A major criticism of many 'diagnostic' normative tests is that their reliability or validity is inadequate.   22

2.7 An inadequate test is likely to produce both false positives and false negatives.   23

2.8 No. Profile analysis of WISC-R scores should be interpreted with considerable caution.   24

2.9 Indeed not. Matching input to modality preference has recurrently been found to make little difference to achievement.   24

2.10 The nature of the task, or the instructional procedure used.   24

Review Three   **Page reference**

3.1 Demonstration of rules by the teacher.   31

3.2 Normally it would begin from a target activity. However, it is conceivable that this might be highlighted in the first instance by the performance of a particular child.   29

3.3 By stating exactly *what* should be done and *how well* the children have to do it.   32

3.4 Definitely not.   34

3.5 Not if smooth learning progress is required.   34

3.6 No. This would demand a level of performance which the child would be most unlikely to possess.   34

3.7 Yes, in any situation where mastery is considered important and this level has not been reached.   35

3.8 Not really, since test profiles do not usually represent direct measurements of skills relevant to the programme.   29

3.9 It is heavily concerned with explicit change, as   32
the things that children do are taken to provide
indications of the rules by which they are
operating.
3.10 Principles of instruction.   29

Review Four   **Page reference**

4.1 It is desirable to take previously taught material   38
into account to promote rapid success on new
tasks.
4.2 Transfer will be strongest between similar items,   38
i.e. it is a function of the amount of similarity
between successive items.
4.3 Shifts in child performance are likely to be most   41
efficacious – children do not necessarily think
and respond as we naïve adults might expect!
4.4 High initial accuracy levels exercise a longer-   41
lasting effect.
4.5 *Production* responses should only be taught   44
when *Identification* is established.
4.6 Overt activity should come first, so that it   49
becomes apparent just what the child can do.
4.7 Consistency comes from presenting the same   49
operations in the same way.
4.8 The least confusing presentation is one which   50
teaches confusable items quite separately.
4.9 The more effective strategy is that of initial   51
teaching plus review.
4.10 A combination of these two variables is likely to   47
be more powerful than either one used separately.

Review Five   **Page reference**

5.1 The modes are either telling or questioning; the   54
elements are either generality or instance.
5.2 Juxtaposition of positive and negative examples.   58
5.3 Least errors would derive from a presentation   57
which admits of a single interpretation.
5.4 Most certainly not.   57

5.5   No. Positive examples alone are not sufficient   57
for this purpose.

5.6   Yes, you could, provided that examples were   58
carefully chosen.

5.7   When the communication is systematically   61
matched to each type of example, i.e. in some
way different for positive examples than it is for
negative examples.

5.8   No. Evidence of *learning* must be derived from a   61
test of the child's capacity to respond appropriately to positive and negative examples of the
concept taught.

5.9   They help to delineate just what it is that a child   62
has learned.

5.10 The *minimum* difference pairs are: flask and   —
flash; crush and crust; also mush and much.
Only a single letter-sound is varied in each pair.

Review Six   **Page reference**

6.1   Any three items from: identification, discrimina-   69
tion, production or sequencing errors.

6.2   The extent of the discrepancy between them.   72

6.3   The nature of the rules by which the child   72
operates.

6.4   It can help to discriminate between correct and   72
error responses, can offer an accurate working
model to follow, and provide for practice activity.

6.5   In the number of error types occurring.   76

6.6   A systematic error.   76

6.7   Just say the name correctly and ask him to try it   77
again.

6.8   The elaborated correction gives a reason for   74
changing a response, in addition to the correct
form of that response. A simple correction only
provides the latter.

6.9   Highlight the differences between the dissimilar   77
items and ask the child to try again.

6.10 Model the whole response, then ask the child to   77
shadow your activity, and finally let him try
alone.

Review Seven   **Page reference**

7.1 Any three of the following: high levels of   83
consistency, freedom from fatigue effects, perfect
recall and accurate record keeping.

7.2 Any two of the following: lack of perception, 83
rigidity of operation, reproduction of program
errors and rejection of alternative responses
outside of a narrow range.

7.3 Drill-and-practice to establish new skills.   86

7.4 Any three of the following: modelling, practice, 86
correction and recording procedures.

7.5 By providing multiple points of entry.   87

7.6 Probably by transferring attention to other things. 87

7.7 Any three items from FASTCHECK 28.   88

7.8 Questions may be given an indefinite number of 89
repeats following an error response.

7.9 Corrective feedback. The Rouse and Evans   89
study found that drill-and-practice, as such,
increased both correct *and* error response rates.

7.10 An increased frequency of deliberate errors on 91
the part of the learner, as he would be receiving
greatest reinforcement for being wrong.

Review Eight   **Page reference**

8.1 A *rate* measurement incorporates speed of res- 95
ponse as well as accuracy, thus offering a more
powerful index of proficiency.

8.2 It should be critical for the increase of academic 97
competence *and* compatible with the child's
existing skills level.

8.3 It will help you to judge when the child's   99
proficiency is increasing more easily than when
a number of differing responses is allowed.

8.4 No. It is important to find out just what he can 102
do for himself at this stage.

8.5 Both *correct* and *error* responses.   103

8.6 Tim's rate of responding to fifty-two letters per 104
minute correct, and three letters per minute
error. Remember that it is necessary to end up
with *rate per minute* in each case.

8.7 Write the rates in *ascending* order and circle the central item.   109

8.8 Any four from: minimal change, time available, adult comparison, peer comparison, and self-comparison.   114

8.9 Accuracy, for without this there can be no fluency later.   117

8.10 The *target rates* will have been achieved and held for three consecutive days.   123

References

Ager, A. (1985) 'Recent developments in the use of micro-computers in the field of mental handicap: implications for psychological practice', *Bulletin of The British Psychological Society*, 38, 142–5.

Ainscow, M. and Tweddle, D.A. (1979) *Preventing Classroom Failure: An Objective Approach*, Chichester, John Wiley.

Ainscow, M. and Tweddle, D.A. (1984) *Early Learning Skills Analysis*, Chichester, John Wiley.

Anderson, L.W. (1984) *Time and School Learning*, London, Croom-Helm.

Anderson, N., Kaufman, A.S. and Kaufman, N.L. (1976) 'The use of the WISC-R with a learning-disabled population: some diagnostic implications', *Psychology in the Schools*, 13(4), 381–6.

Ansubel, D.P. (1968) *Educational Psychology: A Cognitive Science Perspective*, New York, Holt, Rinehart & Winston.

Arter, J.A. and Jenkins, J.R. (1977) 'Examining the benefits and prevalence of modality considerations in special education', *Journal of Special Education*, 11(3), 281–98.

Arter, J.A. and Jenkins, J.R. (1979) 'Differential diagnosis – prescriptive teaching: a critical appraisal', *Review of Educational Research*, 49(4), 517–55.

Behrmann, M. (1984) *Handbook of Microcomputers in Special Education*, Windsor, N.F.E.R.

Bell, M.E. (1985) 'The role of instructional theories in the evaluation of microcomputer courseware', *Educational Technology*, 25(3), 36–40.

Bell, P. and Kerry, T. (1982) *Teaching Slow Learners in Mixed Ability Classes*, London, MacMillan.

Bender, L. (1938) *A Visual-Motor Gestalt Test and its Clinical Use*, New York, American Orthopsychiatric Association.

Bender, M., Valletutti, P. and Bender, R. (1976) *Teaching the Moderately and Severely Handicapped* (vol. III), Baltimore, University Park Press.

Berk, R.A. (1983) 'The Value of WISC-R Profile Analysis for the Differential Diagnosis of Learning-Disabled Children', *Journal of Clinical Psychology* 39(1), 133–6.

Beyer, B.K. (1984) 'Improving thinking skills – defining the problem', *Phi Delta Kappan* (March issue), 486–90.

Blankenship, C. and Lilley, M.S. (1981) *Mainstreaming Students with Learning and Behaviour Problems*, (Evaluation Comment 1:2), London, Holt, Rinehart & Winston.

Bloom, B.S. (1968) *Learning for Mastery*, New York, McGraw-Hill.

Bloom, B.S. (1980) 'The new direction in educational research: alterable variables', *Phi Delta Kappan* (February issue), 382–5.

Branwhite, A.B. and Levey, B. (1982) 'Teacher-controlled learning: an orientation for the 1980s', *Remedial Education* 17(2), 79–83.

Branwhite, A.B. and Becker, R.A. (1982) 'A more direct empirical model for evaluating educational performance', *Educational Review*, 34(1), 47–52.

Brian, R. (1983) 'Sequencing instruction: a cognitive science perspective', *Programmed Learning and Educational Technology*, 20(2), 102–14.

Brophy, J., Rohrkemper, M., Rashid, H. and Goldberger, M. (1983) 'Relationships between teachers' presentation of classroom tasks and student engagement in those tasks', *Journal of Educational Psychology*, 75(4), 544–52.

Brophy, J. and Evertson, C. (1977) *Learning from Teaching: A Developmental Perspective*, Boston, Allyn & Bacon.

Bryant, P.E. and Bradley, E. (1979) 'A psychological view of an educational problem and an educational view of a psychological controversy', *Westminster Studies in Education*, 2, 67–74.

Carnine, D.C. and Silbert, J. (1979) *Direct Instruction Reading*, Columbus, Ohio, Charles E. Merrill.

Cohen, S.A. (1973) 'Minimal brain dysfunction and practical matters such as teaching kids to read', *Annals of the New York Academy of Sciences*, 205, 251–61.

Coopersmith, S. and Feldman, R. (1974) *Fostering a Positive Self-Concept and High Self-Esteem in the Classroom*, New York, Harper & Row.

Darch, C. and Gersten, R. (1985) 'The effects of teacher presentation rate and praise on learning disabled students' oral reading performance', *British Journal of Educational Psychology*, 55, 295–303.

Department of Education and Science (1983) *Assessments and Statements of Special Educational Needs* (Circular 1/83), HMSO.

Desforges, C. and McNamara, D. (1979) 'Theory and practice: methodological procedures for the objectification of craft knowledge', *British Journal of Teacher Education*, 5(2), 145–52.

Eaton, M.D. (1978) 'Data decisions and evaluation', in Haring, N.G., Lovitt, T.C., Eaton, M.D. and Hanson, C. (1978) *The Fourth R: Research in the Classroom*, Columbus, Ohio, Charles E. Merrill.

Emmer, E. and Evertson, C. (1980) *Effective Classroom Management at the Beginning of the Year in Junior High School Classrooms* (Report No. 6107), Austin, Research and Development Center for Teacher Education, University of Texas.

Emmer, E. Evertson, C. and Anderson, L. (1980) 'Effective Classroom Management at the Beginning of the School Year', *Elementary School Journal*, 80(5), 219–31.

Engelmann, S. (1977) 'Sequencing cognitive and academic tasks', in Kneedler, R.D. and Tarver, S.G. *Changing Perspectives in Special Education*, Columbus, Ohio, Charles E. Merrill.

Engelmann, S. and Carnine, D. (1982) *Theory of Instruction: Principles and Applications*, New York, Irvington Publishers.

Feuerstein, R., Rand, Y., Hoffman, M.B. and Miller, R. (1980) *Instrumental Enrichment: An Intervention Program for Cognitive Modifiability*, Baltimore, University Park Press.

Filby, N.N. and Cahen, L.S. (1977) *Teaching Behaviour and Academic Learning Time in the A-B Period: Technical Note V(1b)*, San Francisco, Far West Laboratory for Educational Research and Development.

Fisher, C.W., Filby, N.N., Marliave, R., Cahen, L.S., Dishaw, M.M., Moore, J.E. and Berliner, D.C. (1978) *Teaching Behaviours, Academic Learning Time, and Student Achievement: Final Report of Phase III B, Beginning Teacher Evaluation Study*, San Francisco, Far West Laboratory for Educational Research and Development.

Forness, S.R. and Kavale, K.A. (1985) 'Effects of class size on attention, communication, and disruption of mildly mentally retarded children', *American Educational Research Journal*, 22(3), 403–12.

Frostig, M. and Horne, D. (1964) *The Frostig Programme for the Development of Visual Perceptions* (Teacher's Guide), Chicago, Follett.

Gagné, R.M. (1977) *The Conditions of Learning*, New York, Holt, Rinehart & Winston.

Gardner, J. and Tweddle, D.A. (1979) 'Some guidelines for sequencing objectives', *Association of Educational Psychologists Journal*, 5(2), 23–30.

Glass, G.V. and Smith, M.L. (1978) 'Meta-analysis of research on class size and pupil achievement', *Educational Evaluation and Policy Analysis*, 1(1), 2–16.

Good, T.L. and Beckermann, T.M. (1978) 'Time on task: a naturalistic study in sixth-grade classrooms', *Elementary School Journal*, (1978), 193–201.

Good, T.L. and Brophy, J.E. (1984) *Looking in Classrooms*, London, Harper & Row.

Harzem, P., Lee, I., and Miles, T.R. (1976) 'The effects of pictures on learning to read', *British Journal of Educational Psychology*, 46(3), 318–22.

Hayes, D.A. and Readence, J.E. (1983) 'Transfer of learning from illustration-dependent text', *Journal of Educational Research*, 76(4), 245–8.

Hickey, K. (1977) *The Dyslexia Language Training Programme*, London, Hickey.

Hirschoren, A. and Kavale, K. (1976) 'Profile analysis of the WISC-R', *The Exceptional Child*, 23(2), 83–7.

Houghton, E.C. (1980) 'Practising practices: learning by activity', *Journal of Precision Teaching*, 1(3), 3–20.

Johnson, S.W. and Morasky, R.L. (1980) *Learning Disabilities*, London, Allyn & Bacon.

Jenkins, J.R. and Pany, D. (1978) 'Standardised achievement tests: how useful for special education?' *Exceptional Children*, 44(6), 448–53.

Kavale, K. (1981) 'Functions of the ITPA: are they trainable?' *Exceptional Children*, 47, 496–510.

Kavale, K. and Forness, S. (1985) *The Science of Learning Disabilities*, Windsor, NFER.

Kearsley, G.P. and Frost, J. (1985) 'Design factors for successful video-disc-based instruction', *Educational Technology*, 25(3), 7–13.

Kiernan, C. (1981) *Analysis of Programmes for Teaching*, Basingstoke, Globe Education.

Kirk, S., McCarthy, L. and Kirk, W. (1968) *The Illinois Test of Psycholinguistic Abilities* (rev. edn), Urbana, Illinois, University of Illinois Press.

Klausmeier, H.J. and Goodwin, W. (1975) *Learning and Human Abilities*, New York, Harper & Row.

Koenig, C.H. and Kunzelmann, H.P. (1980) *Classroom Learning Screening*, Columbus, Ohio, Charles E. Merrill.

Kounin, J.S. and Gump, P.V. (1974) 'Signal systems of lesson settings and task related behaviour of pre-school children', *Journal of Educational Psychology*, 66, 555–62.

Kunzelmann, H.P., Cohen, M.A., Hulton, W.J., Martin, G.L. and Mingo, A.R. (1971) *Precision Teaching*, Seattle, Special Child Publications.

Larsen, S., Parker, R. and Hammill, D. (1982) 'Effectiveness of psycholinguistic training: a response to Kavale', *Exceptional Children*, 50(1), 54–60.

Leon, J.A. and Pepe, H.J. (1985) 'Self instructional training: cognitive behaviour modification for remediating arithmetic defects', *Exceptional Children*, 50(1), 54–60.

Levey, B., Branwhite, A.B. and Peterson, M. (1985) *The Precision Phonics Programme*, National Association for Remedial Education, Stafford, in press.

Liberty, K.A. (1975) 'Data decision rules' (unpublished paper), University of Washington, Experimental Education Unit.

Lilley, M.S. (1979) *Children with Exceptional Needs: A Summary of Special Education*, New York, Holt, Rinehart & Winston.

Mann, L. (1971) 'Psychometric phrenology', *Journal of Special Education*, 5, 3–14.

Markle, S.M. and Tiemann, P.W. (1970) *Really Understanding Concepts: Or in Fruminous Pursuit of the Jabberwock* (3rd edn), Champaign, Illinois, Stipes Publishing Co.

Medley, D.W. (1979) 'The effectiveness of teachers', in Peterson, P.L., and Walberg, H.J. (eds) *Research on Teaching*, Berkeley, California, McCutchen.

Merrill, M.D., Kowallis, T. and Wilson, B.G. (1981) 'Instructional design in transition', in Farley, F.H. and Gordon, N.J. *Psychology and Education: The State of the Union*, Berkeley, California, McCutchen.

Miller, J.F. (1985) 'Computer applications in language teaching: software review', *Child Language Teaching and Therapy*, 1(1), 103–9.

Newcomer, P., Larsen, S.C. and Hammill, D.D. (1975) 'A Response to Research on Psycholinguistic Training', *Exceptional Children*, 42, 144–8.

Quattrochi, M. and Sherrets, S. (1980) 'WISC-R: the first five years', *Psychology in the Schools*, 17, 297–312.

Roehler, L. and Duffy, G. (1981) 'Classroom teaching is more than opportunity to learn', *Journal of Teacher Education*, 32(6), 7–11.

Rosenshine, B.V. (1979) 'Direct instruction for skill mastery', Paper presented at the School of Education, University of Milwaukee, Wisconsin.

Rostron, A. and Sewell, D. (1984) *Microtechnology and Special Education*, London, Croom-Helm.

Rouse, M.D. and Evans, P.L. (1985) 'Drill and practice computer programs do improve performance in arithmetic – or do they?' *Remedial Education*, 20(2), 59–63.

Savage, V. and Millar, T. (1976) *Learning to Listen*, Wisbech, Learning Development Aids.

Siegel, P.S. and Crawford, K.A. (1983) 'Two-year follow-up study of discrimination learning by mentally retarded children', *American Journal of Mental Deficiency*, 88(1), 76–8.

Simpson, M. and Arnold, B. (1983) 'Diagnostic tests and criterion referenced assessments: their contribution to the resolution of pupil learning difficulties', *Programmed Learning and Educational Technology*, 20(1), 36–42.

Solomon, D. and Kendall, A.J. (1979) *Final Report on Individual Characteristics and Children's Performance in Varied Educational Settings*, Chicago, Spencer Foundation.

Sternberg, L. and Taylor, R.L. (1982) 'The significance of psycholinguistic training', *Exceptional Children*, 49(3), 254–6.

Stevens, R. and Rosenshine, B.V. (1981) 'Advances in research on teaching', *Exceptional Education Quarterly* (July issue), 1–9.

Strain, P.E. and Shores, R.E. (1983) 'A reply to misguided mainstreaming', *Exceptional Children*, 50(3), 371–2.

Stones, E. (1983) 'Perspectives in pedagogy', *Journal of Education for Teaching*, 9(1), 68–76.

Swann, W. (1983) 'Curriculum principles for integration', in Booth, T. and Potts, P. *Integrating Special Education*, Oxford, Blackwell.

Tarver, S.G. (1978) 'Modality preference and the teaching of reading', *Journal of Learning Disabilities*, 11(1), 17–29.

Torgesen, J.K. (1979) 'What shall we do with psychological processes?', *Journal of Learning Disabilities*, 12(8): 16–23.

Walkin, L. (1982) *Instructional Techniques and Practice*, Cheltenham, Stanley Thorne Publishers.

White, R.T. (1973) 'Research into learning hierarchies', *Review of Educational Research*, 43(3), 361–75.

Wragg, T. (1984) 'The classroom in focus', *Times Educational Supplement*, 24 February, 21.

Wepman, J.M. (1973) *The Wepman Auditory Discrimination Test* (2nd edn), Chicago, Lang Research Associates.

Ysseldyke, J.E., Algozzine, B., Regan, R. and Potter, M. (1980) 'Technical adequacy of tests used by professionals in simulated decision-making', *Psychology in the Schools*, 17, 202–9.

Recommended further reading

Books

Ainscow, M. and Tweddle, D. (1984) *Early Learning Skills Analysis*, Chichester, John Wiley.

Blankenship, C. and Lilly, M.S. (1981) *Mainstreaming Students with Learning and Behaviour Difficulties*, London, Holt, Rinehart & Winston.

Booth, T. and Potts, P. (1983) *Integrating Special Education*, Oxford, Blackwell.

Engelmann, S. and Carnine, D. (1982) *Theory of Instruction: Principles and Applications*, New York, Irvington Publishers Inc.

Formentin, T. and Csapo, M. (1980) *Precision Teaching*, Vancouver, Centre for Human Resources and Development.

Haring, N.G. and Schiefelbusch, R.L. (1977) *Teaching Special Children*, New York, McGraw-Hill.

Howell, K.W., Kaplan, J.S. and O'Connell, C.Y. (1979) *Evaluating Exceptional Children: A Task Analysis Approach*, Columbus, Ohio, Charles E. Merrill.

Kavale, K. and Forness, S. (1985) *The Science of Learning Disabilities*, Windsor, NFER.

Rostron, A. and Sewell, D. (1984) *Microtechnology and Special Education*, London, Croom Helm.

Journal articles

Branwhite, A.B. and Becker, R.A. (1982) 'A more direct empirical model for evaluating educational skills', *Educational Review*, 34(1), 47–52.

Lovitt, T.C. (1975) 'Applied behaviour analysis and learning difficulties, part II; research recommendations and suggestions for practitioners', *Journal of Learning Disabilities*, 8(8), 504–18.

Matthews, C.F. and Booth, S.R. (1982) 'Precision teaching; or how to find out if your teaching is effecting without waiting a term or even a year', *Remedial Education*, 17, 4–7.

McGuigan, C.A. (1980) 'Analysis and use of performance data', *British Columbia Journal of Special Education*, 4(4), 335–53.

Raybould, E.C. and Solity, H.E. (1982) 'Teaching with precision', *Special Education Forward Trends*, 9(2), 9–13.

Glossary of terms

ABILITY: The capacity to function appropriately, bestowed by covert psychological processes which some researchers view as the foundation of human performance.

AFFECTIVE EDUCATION: Teaching concerned with helping children to recognize, label, and communicate feelings.

AIM STAR: A symbol used to represent *target rates* of performance on a Progress Chart.

AUDITORY DISCRIMINATION: The facility to distinguish between sound inputs which have differing physical characteristics.

BASELINE LEVEL: The quality of performance which a child produces on his own before some form of teaching intervention is commenced.

COMPETENCY: A clearly exhibited capacity to perform a skill proficiently.

COMPUTER PROGRAM: The information coded on to audio-tape, floppy disc, cartridge or ROM-chip which directs the computer to carry out certain precise functions.

CONCEPT: A set of ideas which share at least one common attribute.

CORRECT RESPONSE: One in which the child reproduces all the essential characteristics of a model response provided by the teacher.

CORRELATION: A statistical relationship between events occurring in association with each other, not implying that one makes the other happen.

COVERT RESPONSE: One which cannot be directly observed, such as the thinking out of an answer to a written question.

CUE: A sound, action, or symbol providing a stimulus to appropriate action on the part of the child.

DISCRIMINATION: The faculty to detect differences between any items which are not identical with each other.

ELABORATED FEEDBACK: Information given following an incorrect response, which gives a child the reason why the response was incorrect and provides the correct form of the response concerned.

EMPIRICAL EVALUATION: A form of investigation which is guided by direct experience or experiment for which observational data are collected.

ERROR RESPONSE: One in which the child fails to produce the minimum level of performance necessary to respond correctly.

FEEDBACK: Information given to a child in order to help improve his or her performance. Typically this involves positive feedback relating to features which are accurate, and negative feedback relating to aspects which it is desirable to change.

GOAL: An agreed end towards which effort is directed.

HARDWARE: The equipment which constitutes a computer system, e.g. the computer, disc-drive, VDU, printer, concept-board, etc.

IDENTIFICATION RESPONSE: One which involves the selection of a correct option from a provided set of alternatives.

INPUT: Numbers, letters, words or abstract symbols keyed into the computer by the person operating the hardware. Also a particular type of stimulation used to help a child learn.

INSTRUCTION: The verbal and behavioural process of imparting educational information.

LINE OF PROGRESS: The line drawn to connect data points on a Progress Chart to highlight changes in the child's performance.

MASTERY: A quality of responding which is often rapid as well as consistently accurate.

MEDIAN VALUE: The value which represents the half-way point in an array of performance data.

MODALITY: A learning modality is often taken to be synonymous with the particular sensory channel through which teaching input is received.

MODEL RESPONSE: One that exhibits all the essential features of correct performance.

NEGATIVE EXAMPLE: An example which does not bear out the rule taught, one that violates the rule.

OBJECTIVE: A stated activity which carries the learner forward towards the final goal.

OVERT RESPONSE: One that can easily be seen or otherwise detected by an observer.

PERCEPTUAL MOTOR ABILITY: A general capacity to transform stimuli received through various sensory channels into a related set of motor activities.

POSITIVE EXAMPLE: An example which is consistent with the rule taught, and which reflects the rule in exemplary fashion.

PRECISION TEACHING: An orientation which emphasizes the need for continuous measurement of classroom performance.

PRODUCTION RESPONSE: One which has to be based on unaided recall of information.

PSYCHOLINGUISTIC ABILITY: A general capacity to process and generate information in verbal terms.

PSYCHOLOGICAL PROCESSES: Those which involve information-processing functions within the central nervous system.

RECALL: The capacity to retrieve information from memory without assistance.

RECOGNITION: The capacity to identify a given item from a number of options.

RELIABILITY: The technical capacity of a test to cover repeatedly the same ground or to assess the same features of a learner's performance recurrently. This is a bit like being able to drive your car into various parking spaces.

REMEDIAL LOOP: A cycle of teaching which takes a child

out of a learning programme in order to overcome a recurrent error, and which prepares him or her for a return to the programme afterwards.

RESPONSE: The production by a child of any word or action which follows from previous teaching input.

SEQUENCE: A related series of items following one another in succession.

SKILL: A type of performance implying previous learning and practice.

SOFTWARE: The range of programs available to shape the computer's operations.

TRANSFER OF LEARNING: The application of skill across like tasks or situations, for example, reading the time off a school clock as well as a wristwatch.

TUTOR: A proficient third party who is employed to provide instruction, perhaps another adult or an older child.

VALIDITY: The technical capacity of a test to cover the most important features of the learner's performance repeatedly. This is like being able to park your car in your own garage consistently, rather than just in any garage.

VISUAL PERCEPTION: The capacity to receive and understand visual information.

Author index

Subject index